Rebecca

A play

Adapted from Daphne du Maurier's play
by Clifford Williams

Samuel French — London
New York - Toronto - Hollywood

REBECCA

This revised verison of *Rebecca* was first performed at the Churchill Theatre, Bromley, on 20th February 1990, with the following cast:

Frith	Robert Gladwell
Beatrice Lacy	Jane Lowe
Giles Lacy	David Weston
Frank Crawley	Richard Clifford
Maxim de Winter	Clive Arrindell
Mrs de Winter	Helena Michell
Mrs Danvers	Pauline Jameson
Robert	Nick Bailey
Jack Favell	Julian Fellowes
Colonel Julyan	Leon Eagles
William Tabb	Ray Llewellyn
Servant	Jean Murphy

Directed by Clifford Williams
Designed by Tim Goodchild
Lighting by Kevin Sleep

CHARACTERS

Frith
Beatrice Lacy
Giles Lacy
Frank Crawley
Maxim de Winter
Mrs de Winter
Mrs Danvers
Robert
Jack Favell
Colonel Julyan
William Tabb
Servants

The action of the play takes place in the hall of Manderley, home of Maxim de Winter, some years before the Second World War

REBECCA

The original version of *Rebecca* was first performed at the Opera House, Manchester, on March 11th, 1940, with the following cast:

Frith	Clive Woods
Mrs Danvers	Margaret Rutherford
Beatrice Lacy	Edith Sharpe
Giles Lacy	George Thorpe
Frank Crawley	Raymond Huntley
Robert	Peter Hicks
First Maid	Grace Denbeigh-Russell
Second Maid	Isolde Denham
Maxim de Winter	Owen Nares
Mrs de Winter	Celia Johnson
Jack Favell	Ronald Ward
Second Footman	Theodore Meade
Mr Coleman Fortescue	Ernest Hare
Mrs Coleman Fortescue	Dorothy Lane
Colonel Julyan	C.V. France
William Tabb	Richard George

Directed by George Devine

ACT I

SCENE 1

*The hall of Manderley, the country home of Maxim de Winter. Early evening.
May 7th. The 1930s*

*There are double doors at the back of the hall. When open, these reveal an
outer hall which gives access to the front door (off) and other parts of the
house. A table is visible in the outer hall*

*To one side of the double doors there is a fireplace, with an alabaster vase
and several ornaments on the mantelpiece above it; nearby is a bell-push.
Beyond the fireplace, french windows lead to a terrace and lawns*

*To the other side of the central doors there is another, single door and a
staircase leading to a landing and archway. Beyond the archway are unseen
corridors and rooms*

*The hall is elegantly furnished. The furniture includes: a large settee,
armchairs, tables (one of which is a drinks table) and a grand piano. A
telephone stands on one of the tables, a box of cigarettes on another*

As the CURTAIN *rises, the hall is empty. Its double doors are open. The stable
clock is striking six (off). The doorbell rings. Frith crosses the outer hall.
Voices are heard. Beatrice, Giles and Frith enter the hall through the double
doors* C

Beatrice Any idea what time they are arriving, Frith?
Frith Mr de Winter said on the telephone we were to expect them any time
after six, madam. The stable clock has just struck.
Beatrice We shall certainly wait, then; it would be such a pity to miss them
now.
Frith Have you had tea, madam?
Beatrice Yes, thank you, Frith.
Frith Whisky and soda, sir?
Giles Not a bad idea.
Beatrice The Major will wait until Mr de Winter arrives.
Frith Very good, madam. I expect Mr Crawley will be up from the office
directly. I will tell him you are here.

Beatrice Thank you, Frith.

Frith exits C

Giles I suppose you haven't forgotten we're dining with the Cartwrights?
Beatrice I don't care a damn about the Cartwrights. I want to see the bride.
Giles Maxim may not thank us particularly for barging in on their first
evening at home.
Beatrice Well, I don't care. I am curious. Maxim of all people throwing his
cap over the mill in this extraordinary way.
Giles A very good thing for Maxim that he has married again.
Beatrice Yes. One hopes so. (*She walks to the french windows and looks
out*) Funny how it gets one, this place, whenever one comes home. Never
changes, never lets one down.
Giles I wouldn't say it hadn't changed. What about when your father was
alive? All the Victorian furniture and those ghastly rockeries all over the
lawns.
Beatrice Yes, Rebecca got rid of them. She did wonders with the garden and
the house. My heavens, she was clever ... When Frith showed us in just
now, it was the first thing that struck me. Everything just the same, as
though she were still here, as though — if one looked up — she would come
running down those stairs.
Giles Bee!
Beatrice Sorry ——

Frank Crawley enters through the french windows

Hallo, Frank!
Frank How do you do, Mrs Lacy. (*He shakes hands with Beatrice and Giles*)
I didn't realize you were here.
Giles How are you, Crawley?
Frank Would either of you like a drink?
Beatrice We're waiting till they arrive. Do you know anything about her at
all, Frank? All we had was a wire from Maxim the day he got married, and
a postcard from Venice a fortnight ago, saying she was twenty-one and
paints. Has he been more forthcoming to you?
Frank He wrote me a line or two — yes. Didn't say very much, but then he
never does.
Beatrice Are you pleased?
Frank Why, yes, aren't you?
Beatrice Yes — yes, I suppose so. It depends on the girl rather, doesn't it?
Frank Yes, of course.
Giles I think it's rather a pity he brought her back here so soon. They ought
to have gone round the world or something. Gone on a cruise.

Beatrice My dear Giles, can you see Maxim on a cruise? What nonsense!
Giles Hang it all, why not? See Florida, Honolulu, all those places.
Beatrice Speaking as the world's worst sailor, I can't say a honeymoon at
sea would appeal to me. Giles and I went to Switzerland and then we had
twelve hours on end in a *wagon-lit*. Remember, Giles?
Giles Am I likely to forget?
Beatrice My theory is that she's either a dazzling beauty or a blasted blue-
stocking. She might possibly be an ex-chorus girl. Monte Carlo is lousy
with 'em.
Frank I can satisfy your mind on that. Maxim did tell me in his letter she had
no relatives and was acting as companion to an American woman.
Beatrice My God! She probably wears spectacles and trims her own hats.
Frank I don't see why. My sister was a companion to an old lady for many
years.

Frith enters C

Frith They've rung up from the lodge, sir, to say the car has just passed
through the gates.
Frank Thank you, Frith.
Beatrice I believe you're as excited as I am, Frith.
Frith It is rather an event, madam.
Beatrice Are the staff pleased about it?
Frith Oh yes, madam. We all like a wedding.
Beatrice It's an excellent thing for Mr de Winter.
Frith Yes, madam.

Frith exits C

There is the noise of a car drawing up and the car door slamming

Giles Here they come.
Maxim (*off*) Well, here we are, Frith. Everyone well?
Frith (*off*) Yes, sir, thank you. Glad to see you home, and madam, too. Hope
you had a good journey down?
Maxim (*off*) Not so bad.
Frith (*off*) Major and Mrs Lacy are here, sir.

Maxim enters C, followed by Frith

Maxim Bee, I didn't expect to see you. Hallo, Giles! How nice of you both
to come over. Hallo, Frank! Quite a party, eh?

*During the following dialogue, servants can be seen carrying several items
of luggage across the hall*

Beatrice Well, where is she?
Maxim Who? Oh! (*He laughs*) Too scared to come in, I expect. (*He moves back to the doors*) Come on in. It's only Bee and Giles. They won't eat you.

Mrs de Winter enters

First of all, say "How do you do" to Frith, who has known me since I was five years old, and used to put me across his knee and spank me.
Mrs de Winter How do you do. (*She shakes his hand*)
Frith Very glad to see you, madam.
Maxim Where's Mrs Danvers?
Frith Probably attending to the rooms, sir.
Maxim Good. Ask her to come as soon as she can.

Frith exits C

Here is Bee, my one and only sister, who is so itching with curiosity to see you that she's motored fifty miles ——

Mrs de Winter and Beatrice shake hands

—— Giles, my brother-in-law ——

Mrs de Winter and Giles shake hands

—— and Frank Crawley, who thinks he runs the estate, but actually I do the whole thing myself.

Mrs de Winter shakes Frank's hand

Beatrice Well, I must say, you're entirely different from what I expected.
Maxim What did you expect?
Giles A blasted blue stocking.
Maxim You mustn't mind Bee. She believes in speaking her mind.

Frank offers Mrs de Winter a cigarette

Mrs de Winter No, thank you.

Frith enters C *with sherry and Robert with whisky. Beatrice, Mrs de Winter and Frank take sherry. Giles takes a whisky and soda*

Beatrice You must forgive us for thrusting ourselves upon you so soon, but we really couldn't resist it. If you will go and get married in this hole-and-corner fashion, you'll have to put up with a certain amount of curiosity. You're looking better, thank goodness. I suppose we've got you to thank for that. (*She nods at Mrs de Winter*)

Maxim You imagine everyone ill who doesn't look as bloated as Giles.

Beatrice Bosh! You know perfectly well you were a perfect wreck six months ago. Giles, bear me out. Didn't Maxim look perfectly ghastly last time we came over?

Giles Damn good thing you went away.

Mrs de Winter (*shyly*) Maxim's very sunburnt. It hides a multitude of sins. You should have seen him in Venice. Breakfast on the balcony every morning. Trying to get brown on purpose. He thinks it makes him better-looking.

Frank It must have been wonderful in Venice this time of the year.

Mrs de Winter Yes, it was. We found something different every day, a bridge, or a church, or the wall of an old house. I wanted to paint them all, and there was never time. Have you been there, too?

Frank No, unfortunately.

Mrs de Winter Where actually do you live?

Beatrice In Devon, the other side of Launceston. The hunting is so much better with us. You must come over one day when Maxim can spare you. We can mount you.

Mrs de Winter I'm afraid I don't ride.

Beatrice Oh, you must take it up. You can't possibly live in the country and not ride. You won't know what to do with yourself. Painting is very nice, of course, but there's no exercise in it.

Maxim We're not all such fresh air fiends as you, Bee.

Beatrice I wasn't talking to you, old boy. We all know you are perfectly happy sloping about the gardens and never breaking out of a slow walk.

Mrs de Winter I'm very fond of walking too. I'm sure I shall never get tired of rambling about Manderley and I can bathe when it's warmer.

Beatrice My dear, you are an optimist. I can hardly ever remember bathing here. The water is far too cold.

Mrs de Winter I don't mind that, as long as the currents are not too strong. Is the bathing safe in the bay? (*She pauses in embarrassment*)

Giles I say, Bee, we shall have to be hitting the road.

Maxim Oh, must you go?

Beatrice Yes, we're dining with the Cartwrights.

Giles We shall be infernally late as it is.

Beatrice Suppose you go and do something about the car then?

Giles Got a new bus, Maxim. Rather pleased with it. One of those four-and-a-half-litre Lagondas. Complete cad's car. Come and look. You, too, Crawley.

Maxim, Frank and Giles exit C

Beatrice Dear Maxim. He's aching for us to go. I know the signs so well.
I'm devoted to him, you know, although we always bicker like cat and dog
when we meet. You mustn't mind me saying so, but you're even younger
looking than I expected.

Mrs de Winter I'm twenty-one.

Beatrice An absolute child. When you came in just now you could have
knocked me down with a feather. What were you doing down in Monte
Carlo? Companion to some ghastly American? What on earth for?

Mrs de Winter Well, I had to earn my living.

Beatrice Hadn't you any family?

Mrs de Winter No.

Beatrice I see. We are all delighted and I do so hope you'll be happy.

Mrs de Winter Thank you very much.

Beatrice Poor Maxim went through a ghastly time, you know. Let's hope
you've made him forget about it. (*She smiles*) Don't mind me saying so,
but I think you ought to do something to your hair. Why don't you have it
waved? It's so lanky, isn't it? Must look awful under a hat. Try sweeping
it behind your ears.

Mrs de Winter does so

No, that's worse. Too severe. What does Maxim say? Does he think it suits
you?

Mrs de Winter I don't know. He's never talked about it.

Beatrice Oh! Well, don't go by me. Tell me, did you get any clothes in Paris
or London?

Mrs de Winter No, we hadn't any time.

Beatrice I can tell by the way you dress you don't care a hoot what you wear.

Mrs de Winter I do. I'm fond of nice things. I never had much money to
spend on clothes up to now.

Beatrice I wonder Maxim didn't stay a week or so in London to get you
something decent to wear. He's generally so particular.

Mrs de Winter Is he? He never seems particular to me. I don't think he
notices what I wear at all. I don't think he minds.

Beatrice Oh? Oh, he must have changed, then. D'you suppose you'll have
a lot of people down to stay?

Mrs de Winter I don't know. Maxim hasn't said.

Beatrice One never could get a bed in the old days. Tremendous parties.
Somehow I don't quite see you ... Oh, well ... it's a pity you don't ride or
shoot. You miss a lot.

Giles enters the outer hall

Giles (*calling*) Bee, come on!

Beatrice I must be off. What do you want for a wedding present? We must give you something, of course.

Mrs de Winter Oh, please don't bother.

Beatrice Nonsense! I'm not one to grudge you a present even if we weren't asked to your wedding.

Mrs de Winter I hope you didn't mind. Maxim wanted it to be abroad and absolutely quiet.

Beatrice Of course not. Very sensible. After all, he had a terrific show last time. Sorry, my dear. I didn't mean to be rude. I suppose I've said all sorts of things I shouldn't. You see — you are so very different from Rebecca.

Giles enters c

Giles What are you doing? We shall have to drive like stink to make it. (*He moves to Mrs de Winter*) Goodbye, I'm damn glad you married Maxim. Come and stay with us whenever you want to, and bring your paint-box. Heaps of horses in the stables and I'd like pictures of all of 'em.

Mrs de Winter (*smiling*) Goodbye, Giles.

Mrs de Winter and Giles shake hands

Beatrice Bye-bye, my dear.

Mrs de Winter and Beatrice shake hands

Look after Maxim. And if you do go up to London to buy clothes, I'll give you one or two addresses ...

Giles Come on, Bee!

Beatrice and Giles exit c

A pause

Frank enters c

Frank Some more sherry?

Mrs de Winter No, thank you.

Frank Tired?

Mrs de Winter Yes — rather.

Frank This must have been an ordeal for you. I'm so sorry.

Mrs de Winter Do you live near here?

Frank Yes. I have a small house on the estate, which we use as an office. Maxim and I do all our work there.

Mrs de Winter You must be a great comfort to him.
Frank I don't know about that. I love my job, you know. And I'd rather work for Maxim than anyone in the world.

Maxim enters C

Maxim Thank God they've gone. I find a little of my family goes a very long way. What did you think of Bee?
Mrs de Winter I like her. I think she's sincere.
Maxim Sincerity's her strong point. It generally rubs me up the wrong way. I wanted to take you round the garden, and now it's too late. Anything happened, Frank, since I've been away?
Frank No, I don't think so. Young Mitchell has settled down at Tregaminion all right.
Maxim Did you get the roof done for him?
Frank Yes — managed to pick up some really good slate at Delabole. I think you'll like it. Hasn't spoilt the farmhouse a bit.
Maxim We could use it here on the Long Barn in the autumn.
Frank Yes, that's what I thought. (*He smiles at Mrs de Winter*) You won't be interested in all this, Mrs de Winter. I'll see Maxim in the morning.
Maxim Nonsense. She's got to get used to it.
Mrs de Winter Of course.
Frank By the way, Maxim, you're going to be faced with a demand.
Maxim What?
Frank They want you to revive the Fancy-dress Ball.
Maxim Oh, hell!
Frank Yes, I know.
Mrs de Winter What's that, Maxim?
Maxim Oh! One of those infernal institutions that we started some years ago on Midsummer's Eve ... and I've been expected to play up ever since. The locals look upon Manderley as if it were a pavilion on the end of the pier, and one's supposed to do a turn for their benefit.
Frank I think they would enjoy a show of some sort. (*To Mrs de Winter*) We're very conservative down here, you know, about these things, and something should be done in your honour. (*Pause*) Well, it's up to you, Maxim. If you don't feel like facing it ——
Maxim Why the devil shouldn't I face it? As long as I don't have to dress up for the damned thing I don't mind. (*Ironically*) We've only got a bare month, haven't we? Let's start writing out invitations tonight.
Mrs de Winter Can I help at all? I can type, you know.
Frank Don't worry. It can all be done at the office. Licking stamps is the longest job.
Maxim Yes. We'll give you that to do.

Frank Well, I'm not going to worry you any more tonight. You must be longing for a rest. Good-night. (*He shakes hands with Mrs de Winter*)

Mrs de Winter Good-night.

Maxim Hang on. I'll walk down with you. I want to stretch my legs. You don't want to come?

Mrs de Winter No — no, I don't think so.

Frank exits through the french windows

Maxim I won't be long. Don't look so sad. You won't have to worry about the house, you know. Mrs Danvers runs it all; food, staff, every damn thing. You've only got to be yourself. They'll all adore you.

Maxim exits calling "Frank"

Mrs Danvers enters through the upper archway. She walks slowly down the stairs

Mrs Danvers Good-evening, madam. I'm Mrs Danvers.

Mrs de Winter Good-evening. Mr de Winter has told me about you. He said you — you are a very wonderful person, you do so much for Manderley. You will have to show me round when you are not too busy.

Mrs Danvers It's for you to make your own time, madam. Of course I don't know what you and Mr de Winter have arranged. The house has been in my charge now for nearly a year, and Mr de Winter has never complained. It was very different when the late Mrs de Winter was alive ... there was a lot of entertaining then, and though I managed for her she liked to supervize things herself.

Mrs de Winter You must run the house as it has always been run. I don't want to make any changes.

Mrs Danvers Very good, madam. Then I can give orders for things to continue as usual. Breakfast in the dining-room at nine, and the fire lit in the morning-room when cold. Mrs de Winter always did her correspondence in the morning-room after breakfast. On cold days the fire is lit in the library just before tea. If you wish it lit earlier, I will give orders for it to be done.

Mrs de Winter Oh, no. I'm sure I shan't need it any earlier.

Mrs Danvers Alice is unpacking for you now and will look after you until your maid arrives.

Mrs de Winter I haven't got a maid. I'm sure Alice will look after me all right.

Mrs Danvers I'm afraid that would not do for long. It's usual, madam, you know, for ladies in your position, to have a personal maid.

Mrs de Winter If—if you think it's necessary, perhaps you would see about it for me, some young girl, perhaps, wanting to train.

Mrs Danvers Very good, madam.

Mrs de Winter I suppose you have been here at Manderley for many years?

Mrs Danvers Not as long as Frith. Frith was here when Mr de Winter was a boy.

Mrs de Winter Oh! Really.

Mrs Danvers I came here when the late Mrs de Winter was a bride.

Mrs de Winter Oh, I see.

Mrs Danvers If Mr de Winter doesn't like the arrangement of the new wing, he must tell me.

Mrs de Winter I had no idea Mr de Winter was having anything changed. He shouldn't have done it — for me.

Mrs Danvers Mr de Winter said he would prefer it.

Mrs de Winter Oh! Do we see the sea from our rooms?

Mrs Danvers No, you can't hear it, either. They used to live in the west wing when Mrs de Winter was alive, but it hasn't been used since she was drowned. Would you like me to show you your rooms?

Mrs de Winter I think perhaps I'd rather wait till Mr de Winter comes back.

Mrs Danvers Very good, madam.

Mrs de Winter Mrs Danvers, I hope we shall be friends. This sort of life is new to me. And I do want to make a success of it, and above all to make Mr de Winter happy.

Mrs Danvers I shall try and see that everything runs smoothly, madam. Naturally, it is a little difficult for me and the rest of the staff. We were all very devoted to the late Mrs de Winter.

Mrs de Winter Yes — I understand.

Mrs Danvers When we heard that Mr de Winter was to marry again, we could hardly believe it at first, but Mr Crawley explained to us how it was. He said he supposed the empty house had got on Mr de Winter's nerves, and he could not go on living here alone. If there is nothing more at present, I will go and see if Alice has finished. Dinner is at eight o'clock. Good-night, madam.

Mrs de Winter Good-night.

Mrs Danvers exits up the stairs. Maxim comes in through the french windows with some letters

Maxim Hallo! What are you doing huddled there? Regretting Italy already?

Mrs de Winter No, no, of course not.

Maxim It's been a long day. You want your dinner, that's it, isn't it?

Mrs de Winter Yes, I expect so. Where did you go?

Maxim Just down to the office. You mustn't mind, you know, if I'm out a good deal. Running an estate is a full-time job. I don't loaf here like I did on holiday.

Mrs de Winter No, of course not. Beatrice said I was younger than she expected.

Maxim Beatrice can mind her own business.

Mrs de Winter I wish I was ten, fifteen years older. I wish I was dark, and clever, and amusing.

Maxim You wouldn't be with me here now if you were!

Mrs de Winter It's all very well for you. You know everything there is to know about me, but I — why, I scarcely know anything more about you than the day we met.

Maxim And what did you know then?

Mrs de Winter Well — that you lived at Manderley and — and that you had lost your wife.

Maxim I told you in Monte Carlo I didn't want to discuss the past. Those days are finished. I want to begin all over again.

Mrs de Winter Maxim — don't be angry with me.

Maxim I'm not angry with you.

Frith enters c with the evening paper

Frith The evening paper, sir.

Maxim Thank you, Frith.

Frith exits c

Sorry. Having that crowd to meet us was the trouble. I had hoped we should be quite alone. And we could have gone round the grounds together. Nothing ever happens exactly as one plans it, ever. (*He goes to the french windows*) Our bedroom looks out on the rose garden, not this way. It's my favourite view. The first thing I remember is trotting along after my mother, while she nipped off the dead roses. There's something peaceful and happy about that view, and it's quiet, too. You can't hear the sea from there.

Mrs de Winter Yes, that's what Mrs Danvers said.

Maxim Oh, you've met old Danvers? How did you get on?

Mrs de Winter Oh, all right. She was just a little stiff. Perhaps she thought I was going to interfere with the running of the house.

Maxim I don't think she would mind your doing that. Don't worry about her. She's an extraordinary character in many ways. Very efficient though.

Mrs de Winter I expect we shall get on well when she knows me better. After all, it's natural enough that she should resent me a bit at first.

Maxim Why the devil should she?

Mrs de Winter Well, it must be much easier for a housekeeper to look after a man on his own. I daresay she has got used to doing it, and perhaps she's afraid I might be very overbearing.

Maxim Overbearing — my God ... (*He stops, then kisses the top of her head*) Let's forget about Mrs Danvers. What about a bath before dinner? The dressing-gong will be going in a minute. I'm infernally hungry.

Mrs de Winter Maxim — you know just forty-eight hours ago we were having dinner by the Grand Canal. And afterwards we leant over the bridge together and watched the lights, and do you remember the man singing in the square? You gave him all the change in your pockets, and he wished us luck and happiness, and many, many bambini.

Maxim Yes. And he stank of garlic, too. I don't know which was worse. That or the drains in the canal. (*He laughs*) Gosh! It's good to be home again. (*He takes the newspaper and sits to read it*)

Mrs de Winter (*moving slowly to the foot of the staircase*) I don't know the way.

Maxim (*absently*) What? Straight through the archway. The first corridor on the right.

Mrs de Winter Maxim?

Maxim Yes?

Mrs de Winter Do you like my hair?

Maxim Your hair? What on earth do you mean? Of course I like it. What's wrong with it?

Mrs de Winter Oh! Nothing ... I just wondered ...

Maxim How funny you are!

A gong sounds

Mrs de Winter goes up the stairs as ——

—— the CURTAIN *falls*

SCENE 2

Morning. June 23rd

There is a thick white mist outside the french windows. A splendid flower arrangement can be seen on the table in the outer hall

Mrs de Winter enters through the french windows with her arms full of roses

Mrs de Winter (*calling*) Frith — Frith!

Frith enters C

Frith, could you bring me a vase for these roses? I've been out in the mist especially to pick them. They'll look lovely in the drawing-room.

Frith I beg your pardon, madam, but the flowers are already done in both the drawing-room and the library. Mrs Danvers finished the arrangements before breakfast.

Mrs de Winter Oh! Oh, I see. I'm too late, then. These roses won't be needed.

Frith I hardly think they will, madam.

Mrs de Winter Are there no vases left at all?

Frith There may be one or two old ones in the flower-room, madam. I will ask Robert to ascertain.

Frith exits c

Mrs de Winter sees the alabaster vase standing on the mantelpiece. There is nothing in it. She goes across and stands on tiptoe to take it. As she does so her sleeve brushes against an ornament and it falls to the ground and breaks. She picks up the broken pieces of ornament. She wraps them up in a piece of newspaper

Robert enters c *with three vases on a tray*

Robert These are all I could find, madam.

Mrs de Winter Oh, thank you, Robert. Put them on the table, will you? And, Robert, you might just throw away this rubbish. (*She hands him the newspaper with the broken pieces of ornament. She begins putting the roses in the alabaster vase*)

Robert Yes, madam.

Robert exits c

The stable clock strikes ten and a ship's siren is heard in the distance. Mrs de Winter puts more roses in the alabaster vase until it is nearly filled. She stands back, with her head on one side, to see the effect

Frith enters c

Mrs de Winter Frith, could you bring some water for this vase?

Frith Excuse me, madam, but the alabaster vase is never used for flowers.

Mrs de Winter Does it leak?

Frith I couldn't say, madam. I have never seen it moved before. The vase has always stood in the centre of the mantelpiece, madam. It belonged to the late Mrs de Winter.

Mrs de Winter Oh! I see. (*She takes the roses out of the vase*)

Frith Will you be requiring anything else, madam?

Mrs de Winter No, thank you. (*She takes the vases Robert brought in off the tray and puts them on the table*)

Frith exits c

Mrs de Winter picks up the alabaster vase, crosses to the mantelpiece and replaces it

Meanwhile a man — Jack Favell — appears at the french windows

During the following dialogue, Mrs de Winter arranges roses in two of the vases

Favell (*leaning forward and whispering*) Mrs de Winter ... I beg your pardon. I hope I haven't startled you?

Mrs de Winter No, of course not. Mrs de Winter is dead. Can I help you?

Favell (*coming into the hall*) What a shame. I wouldn't have frightened you for the world. I've no business butting in on you like this. Fact is, I've just been to see old Danny — Mrs Danvers, you know.

Mrs de Winter Oh, yes, of course.

Favell I pop in and see her now and again. She's a great pal of mine, and — well, I'll admit it — I felt I simply must come and pay my respects to the bride. I just wanted a glimpse of you, that's all.

Mrs de Winter Thank you.

Favell Dear old Danny! She's so anxious, bless her, not to disturb anyone. She'd be wild with me if she knew. How's Max?

Mrs de Winter He's very well, thank you. We're giving a Fancy-dress Ball this evening so we're all rather busy. I think Maxim is down at the office if you want to see him.

Favell And left his bride all alone. Isn't he afraid someone will come and carry you off?

Mrs Danvers enters c

Hallo, Danny, here we are again. Perhaps you would introduce me?

Mrs Danvers This is Mr Favell, madam.

Mrs de Winter How do you do. Won't you stay to coffee?

Favell Now isn't that a charming invitation. I've been asked to stay to coffee, Danny. I've a good mind to.

Mrs Danvers frowns

Well, perhaps you're right. I suppose I had better be going, hadn't I? Goodbye, Danny, you know where to get in touch with me.

Favell exits through the french windows

Mrs Danvers Excuse me, madam.

She exits c

Favell enters through the french windows

Favell Dear old Manderley. The place hasn't changed much. I suppose Danny sees to that. What a wonderful woman she is.
Mrs de Winter Yes, she's very efficient.
Favell And what do you think of it all? Like being buried down here or are you bored stiff?
Mrs de Winter I like it very much.
Favell Weren't you living somewhere down in the South of France when you and Max met. Monte, wasn't it? I used to know Monte well.
Mrs de Winter Yes, I was in Monte Carlo.
Favell I'd love to have seen Max living it up on the Riviera. Did he meet you one night at the Casino?
Mrs de Winter No.
Favell In other words, what business is it of mine? Well, bye-bye. It's been a lot of fun meeting you and it would be very sporting of you if you didn't mention this little visit of mine to Max. He doesn't exactly approve of me, I'm afraid; I can't think why. And it might get old Danny into trouble.
Mrs de Winter No ... all right.
Favell That's very good of you. Perhaps I'll come and look you up again. Some day when Max isn't at home. I must be off. Enjoy yourself at the dance. Wish I was going to have one with you myself. How long have you been married? Ten weeks, isn't it?
Mrs de Winter Yes.
Favell Jolly, if I'd got a bride of ten weeks waiting for me at home. I'm only a poor lonesome bachelor. Happy days.

He exits through the french windows

A ship's siren is heard

Frank Crawley enters c

Frank It's all right, don't despair, the fog will lift by the evening.
Mrs de Winter Hallo, Frank. I thought you and Max were down at the office.
Frank Maxim's coming up directly — it's as thick out there as a blanket. I say, this is terrific! (*He looks at the flowers in the outer hall*)

Mrs de Winter I didn't do that. It was Mrs Danvers. (*She places the two filled vases on tables*)

Frank Oh, I see!

Mrs de Winter I'm afraid I'm not very good at flowers.

Frank I think you do them very well.

Mrs de Winter (*picking up the remaining vase and arranging the last roses in it*) I suppose last time you gave the Midsummer's Eve Ball ... Rebecca did the flowers?

Frank I'm afraid I can't remember.

Mrs de Winter Frank, that little cottage on the beach. I went into it the other day. Everything inside is mouldy and damp. The curtains — the furniture — shouldn't something be done about it?

Frank (*quietly*) I think if Maxim wanted anything done he would tell me.

Mrs de Winter Are all the things in it ... Rebecca's?

Frank Yes.

Mrs de Winter (*playing with the flowers*) What did she use the cottage for?

Frank Moonlight picnics, and one thing and another.

Mrs de Winter Moonlight picnics must be great fun. Did you ever go to them?

Frank Once or twice.

Mrs de Winter There's a mooring in the water — off the beach.

Frank Yes, her boat was kept on it.

Mrs de Winter Was that the boat she was sailing when she was drowned?

Frank Yes ... it must have capsized and sank out at sea. She was *lost* overboard.

Mrs de Winter Couldn't someone have gone out to her?

Frank Nobody saw it happen. She often went out, alone, like that. She would come back any time of the night, and sleep at the cottage.

Mrs de Winter How long afterwards was it that they found her?

Frank About two months.

Mrs de Winter Where?

Frank Near Salcombe, about forty miles up channel.

Mrs de Winter How did they know it was her? How could they tell?

Frank Maxim went up to Salcombe to identify her.

Mrs de Winter Frank, I know what you're thinking. You think I'm morbid, and curious, in a rather horrid way. It's not that. It's only that — that sometimes I find myself at such a disadvantage. When I go returning calls, I know people are looking me up and down, wondering what sort of a success I'm going to make of it. I can imagine them saying "What on earth does Maxim see in her?" And then, I begin to wonder myself, I begin to doubt, and I have a feeling that I should never have married Maxim, that we're not going to be happy. You see, I know that whenever I meet anyone new, they are all thinking the same thing: how different she is from Rebecca.

Frank Please ...

Mrs de Winter I realize more and more every day that the things I haven't got — oh, all the qualities that mean most in a woman — she had. And it doesn't help, Frank.

Frank I'm sure Maxim would be very worried if he knew you felt like that. We none of us want to bring back the past, Maxim least of all. And it's up to you to lead us away from it. Not to take us back there again.

Mrs de Winter (*putting the remaining vase of flowers on a table*) Frank, we won't ever talk about these things again, but — will you answer me one thing, quite truthfully?

Frank Go on.

Mrs de Winter Tell me ... was Rebecca very beautiful?

Frank Yes, I suppose she was the most beautiful creature I ever saw in my life.

Maxim enters through the french windows

Maxim There you are, Frank. I've been holloa-ing for you for twenty minutes. There's complete chaos with the illuminations.

Frank Sorry. I'm afraid I've been sitting here doing absolutely nothing. (*To Mrs de Winter*) You'll give me a dance this evening, won't you?

Mrs de Winter You shall have as many dances as you like. I shan't dance with anyone except you and Maxim, and perhaps Giles.

Frank Oh, they will all want to dance with the bride.

Mrs de Winter I'm not a bride. I didn't even have a proper wedding. No white dress, or orange blossom, or trailing bridesmaids.

Maxim A grubby coat and skirt and an old scarf tied round your head. (*He laughs*) You ought to have seen her, Frank. Everybody thought she was my daughter. (*He makes a face at her*)

Mrs de Winter I wish you wouldn't treat me as if I were six.

Maxim How do you want to be treated?

Mrs de Winter Like other men treat their wives.

Maxim Knock you about, you mean? (*He laughs*) Come on, tell us what you are going to wear tonight.

Mrs de Winter Don't you worry, I've thought of something.

Frank I'm sure you'll look very nice whatever you wear.

Maxim Handsomely spoken, Frank. You can take her in to supper, if you like.

Frith enters c

Frith Could I speak to you, sir, a moment?

Maxim Yes, of course, Frith, what is it?

Frank Look here, this won't do. I must see to the lights.
Mrs de Winter Let us know if you want any help.

Frank exits C

Maxim What's the matter, Frith?
Frith It's Robert, sir. There has been a slight unpleasantness between him
and Mrs Danvers. Robert is very upset.
Maxim Oh Lord!
Frith Yes sir. It appears Mrs Danvers has accused Robert of having broken
an ornament. Robert denied the accusation most emphatically and has been
to me nearly in tears, sir.
Maxim I didn't know Robert was so sensitive. Well, you had better ask Mrs
Danvers to come here and we'll get to the bottom of it. What ornament was
it, anyway?
Frith The china cupid, sir, from the mantelpiece.
Maxim Oh Lord! That's one of our treasures, isn't it? Tell Mrs Danvers I'll
see her, will you?
Frith Very good, sir.

Frith exits C

Maxim How I loathe servants' rows.
Mrs de Winter Darling, I meant to tell you before ... the fact is, I broke that
cupid just now, when I was doing some flowers.
Maxim You broke it? Well, why didn't you say so when Frith was here?
Mrs de Winter I don't know, I didn't like to, I was afraid he would think me
a fool.
Maxim He'll think you much more of a fool now. You'll have to explain to
him and Mrs Danvers.
Mrs de Winter Oh no, please, Maxim, you tell them. Let me go upstairs.
Maxim Don't be a little idiot. Anyone would think you were afraid of them.
Mrs de Winter I am afraid of them. At least, not afraid, but ...

Frith ushers Mrs Danvers in C

Maxim It's all a mistake, Mrs Danvers. Apparently Mrs de Winter broke the
cupid herself.
Mrs de Winter I'm so sorry, Mrs Danvers. I never realized Robert would
get into trouble.
Mrs Danvers I found the pieces hidden in an old newspaper. I am afraid I
did not understand ...
Maxim Mrs de Winter thought you would put her in prison. All right, Frith,
you can tell Robert to dry his tears.

Frith Very good, sir.

He exits C

Mrs Danvers I will apologize to Robert, of course. It never occurred to me that Mrs de Winter had broken the ornament herself. Perhaps if such a thing should happen again, Mrs de Winter will tell me personally and I will have the matter attended to.

Maxim Naturally. I can't think why she didn't.

Mrs de Winter I was afraid it was valuable.

Maxim That's why you hid the pieces so carefully. (*He laughs*)

Mrs Danvers It's very unfortunate, sir. I don't think we have ever had any serious breakages here before.

Maxim Yes. Well, it can't be helped. Thank you, Mrs Danvers.

Mrs Danvers exits C

Mrs de Winter I'm sorry, darling. It was very careless of me.

Maxim My sweet child, forget it.

Mrs de Winter I ought to have been more careful. Mrs Danvers must be furious with me.

Maxim What the devil has she got to be furious about? It's not her piece of china.

Mrs de Winter No, but she takes such a pride in it all.

Maxim Oh, damn Mrs Danvers! Fancy not getting hold of her when you broke the thing and saying, "Here, Mrs Danvers, get this mended." Instead of which you scrape up the remains in a newspaper and throw them away. Just like a kitchenmaid.

Mrs de Winter I am like a kitchenmaid. I know I am in lots of ways. I know I felt like one when I called on the Bishop's wife the other day.

Maxim If you wore an old skirt like that I'm not surprised.

Mrs de Winter Of course I didn't call on her in an old skirt. And anyway, I don't think much of people who just judge by one's clothes.

Maxim I'm sure the Bishop's wife doesn't care twopence about clothes, but she may have been rather surprised if you sat on the edge of the chair and answered "Yes" and "No" like someone after a job, which is what you did the only time we answered a call together.

Mrs de Winter I can't help being shy.

Maxim I know you can't, sweetheart, but you make no effort to conquer it.

Mrs de Winter That's not very fair. I try every day, every time I meet anyone new. You don't understand. It's all very well for you. You've been brought up to it.

Maxim Rot! It's not a question of bringing up. You don't think I like calling on people, do you? It bores me stiff.

Mrs de Winter I'm not talking of boredom. If I was just bored, it would be different. I hate people looking at me as if I were a prize cow.

Maxim What does it matter if they do? It gives them some interest in life.

Mrs de Winter What a slap in the eye I must be to them. I suppose that's why you married me. You knew I was dull and quiet and inexperienced. No-one could ever gossip about me.

Maxim What do you mean?

Mrs de Winter I — I don't know. I don't mean anything. Why do you look like that?

Maxim What do you know about gossip down here?

Mrs de Winter Nothing. I only said it because — because of something to say.

Maxim Who's been talking to you?

Mrs de Winter No-one. No-one at all.

Maxim Why did you say what you did?

Mrs de Winter I tell you I don't know! It just came into my head. I was angry, cross. I do hate calling on these people. I can't help it. And you criticized me for being shy. I didn't mean it. Really, Maxim, I didn't.

Maxim I wonder if I did a very selfish thing in marrying you.

Mrs de Winter How do you mean?

Maxim I'm not much of a companion to you, am I? Too many years between us. You ought to have waited and then married a boy of your own age.

Mrs de Winter That's ridiculous. You know age doesn't mean anything. Of course we're companions.

Maxim I rushed you into it. I never gave you a chance to think it over.

Mrs de Winter I didn't want to think it over. There was no other choice.

Maxim Are you happy here?

Mrs de Winter Of course I'm happy. I love Manderley. I don't mind calling on people. I just said that to be tiresome. I'll call on people every day if you want me to. I've never for one moment regretted marrying you, you must know that.

Maxim If you say so, then it's all right.

Mrs de Winter No, but you think it too, don't you, darling? It's not just me? We are happy, aren't we?

There is a silence

Well, why don't you answer?

Maxim If you say we are happy, let's leave it at that. Agreed?

Mrs de Winter You say that because you're disappointed in me. You think I'm not right for Manderley.

Maxim Oh, don't talk nonsense. I never said that. It's your imagination.

Mrs de Winter This all began because I broke the china cupid.

Maxim Oh, damn that infernal cupid!
Mrs de Winter Was it very valuable?
Maxim I've really forgotten.
Mrs de Winter Are all the things on the mantelpiece valuable?
Maxim Yes, I believe so.
Mrs de Winter Perhaps — they were put there when you were first married.
Maxim Perhaps they were.
Mrs de Winter I suppose the cupid was put there then?
Maxim Yes. As a matter of fact, I believe it was a wedding present. Rebecca knew a lot about china.
Mrs de Winter I see. That's why it's so precious. I wonder you didn't shut it up safely with all that other china of hers in that cottage on the beach. It reeks of damp in there, but nothing's broken. Perhaps you haven't been there lately?
Maxim No, I haven't! I never go near the bloody place! And if you had my memories you wouldn't want to go there either, or talk about it, or even think about it. (*He turns to the french windows*)
Mrs de Winter Maxim.
Maxim We ought to have stayed in Italy. We ought never to have come back to Manderley.
Mrs de Winter Maxim ... Maxim ...

Maxim exits through the french windows

Mrs de Winter cries

Mrs Danvers enters through the single door. She has a dress box, tied with string, under her arm

Mrs Danvers Something's the matter, madam?
Mrs de Winter I'm all right, thank you, Mrs Danvers.
Mrs Danvers I hope you are not fretting about the cupid, madam. I don't think Mr de Winter will worry about the actual worth of the ornament. It's the sentimental value attached to it. It belonged to the late Mrs de Winter.
Mrs de Winter Yes, I know.
Mrs Danvers I had the care of her when she was a child. She was lovely, lovely as a picture. She was painted, you know, the year before she died. A famous artist did it. The picture hung in the Academy. I understand it was the picture of the year, but Mr de Winter didn't care for it, and wouldn't have it here at Manderley. I suppose he didn't think it did her justice. I hope the flowers are to your satisfaction, madam?
Mrs de Winter Yes, thank you, Mrs Danvers. They're quite wonderful.
Mrs Danvers Alice tells me, madam, that you have done nothing about a costume for the ball tonight.

Mrs de Winter Oh, I have — I'm going to go as a gypsy.

Mrs Danvers I would never have chosen a gypsy, not if I'd been you. Of course, it's none of my business, I know, but there are so many people coming here to see you for the first time. (*She unties the string, and lifts the lid of the box*) I'm interfering, perhaps, but I couldn't help wondering about this. It's old, of course, it's not been worn for over fifty years, but it's all here, quite intact.

Mrs de Winter What is it?

Mrs Danvers There are many things put away in the house that belonged to Mr de Winter's mother, and his grandmother before that. (*She carefully lifts a white dress out of the box*) This dress must have belonged to Mr de Winter's grandmother. Look at the lovely satin. It would fit you, I can see that. A bit of lifting here and there, I could do in a minute.

Mrs de Winter Do you think it would suit me?

Mrs Danvers Yes, of course.

Mrs de Winter It would be a surprise, wouldn't it?

Mrs Danvers Yes.

Mrs de Winter Oh, it must be fifty times better than the gypsy. We must put it back into the box. I don't want anyone to see. (*She folds the dress quickly and replaces it in the box*)

Mrs Danvers Shall I do your hair for you? It will have to be curled, you know, in soft, loose ringlets.

Mrs de Winter Thank you.

Mrs Danvers And when you are dressed, and we've put a little colour on your cheeks, and your hair is all piled on top of your head, then you'll come to the head of the stairs there and show yourself to Mr de Winter, and you'll look like a picture — just like a picture. (*She stares intently at Mrs de Winter*)

Mrs de Winter looks uncomfortable

(*Picking the box up and slowly putting the string round it again*) I'll help you to dress. I'd like to help you to dress.

Mrs de Winter That's very kind of you.

Mrs Danvers You won't say anything about it, then, to Mr de Winter?

Mrs de Winter No, I won't tell anyone at all.

Mrs Danvers Why don't you come upstairs and try on the dress?

Mrs de Winter I — I don't know. I was hoping — I was wondering if Mr de Winter would come back.

Mrs Danvers I expect he's with Mr Crawley. He'll not return till lunchtime. You'll find the hooks of the dress awkward, all by yourself. I did everything for Mrs de Winter, you know. "You look after me better than anyone, Danny", she used to say. "I won't have anyone but you".

Mrs de Winter Danny. She called you Danny?

Mrs Danvers Yes. It was always Danny. I've kept all her things. Even the stockings she wore that day in London for the last time. She'd flung them over the arm of the chair in her bedroom, when she'd changed into her sailing clothes. There was nothing on her body when it was found, you understand. It was weeks later. The rocks and the sea had battered her so she was unrecognizable. I shall always blame myself for the accident. It was my fault for being out. That evening, I'd gone into Kerrith and stayed late, as Mrs de Winter was up in London ... That's why I didn't hurry back. When I came in about half-past nine, I heard she had returned, had some food, and then gone down to the beach. I was worried at once. It was blowing up from the south-west. She would never have gone if I'd been here. She always listened to me. It began to blow very hard just before midnight and she hadn't come back. I went and told Mr de Winter I was worried. "I expect she's spending the night down at the cottage," he said; "she'll be back first thing in the morning." I sat on my bed till half-past five. Then I couldn't wait any longer. I got up and put on my coat and went down to the shore. It was white and misty — like it is today — and the wind had dropped. I saw the buoy there in the water, and the dinghy, but not the boat. You wouldn't think she had been gone now for so long, would you, not the way I keep the rooms. Just as she had them kept. You would think she had just gone out for a little while and would be back again in the evening. I feel her everywhere. You do too, don't you? Sometimes in the corridors, I fancy I hear her just behind me. That quick, light footstep. I could not mistake it, anywhere. Do you think she can see us now? Do you think the dead come back and watch the living?

Mrs de Winter I don't know ...

Mrs Danvers Sometimes I wonder if she comes back here to Manderley and watches you and Mr de Winter together.

There is the sound of a rocket being launched, outside on the shore

Mrs de Winter What was that?

A second rocket

Mrs Danvers They're rockets. From the coast-guard on the cliff. It must mean there's a ship gone ashore there in the bay.

There is the sound of a third rocket

Mrs Danvers exits up the stairs with the box

The CURTAIN *falls*

24

SCENE 3

The same day. About 9.30 p.m.

Lights are lit on the terrace. The hall has been decorated, ready for the Ball.
Frith is fussing in the hall

Frank enters C in an old rugby sweater, trousers, sea boots, and an overcoat

Frank Evening, Frith.
Frith Good-evening, sir.
Frank I'm the first to appear, then?
Frith Yes, sir. Mr de Winter is on the terrace and Madam isn't down yet.
Frank Major and Mrs Lacy not turned up yet?
Frith No, sir. Mrs Lacy rang up to ask how the fog was. I told her it had lifted.
Frank Good! Have the local people been worrying you on the telephone?
Frith There have been one or two calls, sir. I said the crew of the steamer were
  all safe ashore, and if they wanted any information, would they please ring
  up the harbourmaster at Kerrith, as we didn't know any more about it than
  they did.
Frank That's right, Frith. The whole affair is a perfect nuisance. Does
  anybody know whether the ship was badly damaged?
Frith I did have a word with the engineer, sir. I understood the harbourmaster
  sent down a diver to ascertain the damage, but I haven't heard the result.
Frank I see.
Frith Well, sir, if you'll excuse me, I think I will see that everything's in order
  in the supper-room.
Frank Yes, of course, Frith.

Frith exits C

(*Picking up the telephone receiver; into it*) Kerrith three-two, please. ...
Hallo. ... Is that number seven, Esplanade? ... Hallo! Is the harbourmaster
at home? ... Oh, Mrs Searle! Your husband hasn't come back yet? ... No.
I just wondered if there was any further news. ... Yes, it's Mr Crawley
speaking. I understand a diver went down and I wondered ... You haven't
seen your husband since midday! ... Oh, I see. ... Yes, I expect they're pretty
busy. ... All right, Mrs Searle, thank you. I'm at Manderley tonight, and the
office tomorrow morning. ... Yes. (*He replaces the receiver*)

Maxim enters through the french windows in evening dress

Maxim Someone else ringing up about that confounded ship?

Frank No, I just put a call through the harbourmaster. But he's not back yet.
Maxim They're still out there, I expect. It's barely dark yet. I should think
every soul in Kerrith must have been there this afternoon.
Frank Do you think they'll shift her with the spring tides?
Maxim No. Not an earthly chance. She's fast on the reef!
Frank I can't understand what the dickens the fellow was doing so close in.
Maxim Try navigating in a fog. He must have mistaken the bay for Kerrith
Harbour.
Frank It's a damn nuisance, anyway. (*He walks up and down, frowning*)
Maxim What's the matter?
Frank Nothing. (*He glances at his watch*) Time's getting on. I wonder if the
band have finished eating and drinking.
Maxim You're as jumpy as a kitten. Anyone would think we'd never given
a dance here before. Let's hope it will be a failure, and then nobody will
want us to give another.
Frank That's one way of looking at it.
Maxim All right. Go along and snatch the drink from the band, if you're
getting nervous.

Frank exits C, *laughing*

Maxim begins to play the piano

Mrs Danvers appears at the top of the stairs and comes down

Mrs Danvers I beg your pardon, sir. I was just coming down to see that
everything was in order.
Maxim (*rather shortly*) Yes, thank you, Mrs Danvers.
Mrs Danvers I always do my best, sir, to keep everything as it always used
to be. I hope the dance will be a great success, sir.
Maxim Thank you.

Mrs Danvers turns to leave

Wait a minute. (*He stops playing*) Mr Favell was here this morning, wasn't
he?
Mrs Danvers Mr Favell, sir?
Maxim His car was seen in the drive. You can write and tell him to keep away
from Manderley in future. If you want to see him, you can see him outside.
I won't have him inside the gates. You understand? I'm warning you for
the last time. That's all I want to say. (*He plays again*)

Mrs Danvers stares at him a moment, then exits C

Mrs de Winter comes on to the stairs in her dressing-gown

Mrs de Winter Maxim ...

Maxim (*stopping playing and looking up*) Hallo! You ought to be dressed. What are you up to?

Mrs de Winter I want you to throw me up a white rose.

Maxim What do you want a white rose for?

Mrs de Winter Never mind. Throw me one up.

Maxim (*taking a white bud and smelling it*) Come and get it.

Mrs de Winter I can't. Not like this.

Maxim You won't have it, then.

Mrs de Winter Please, Maxim.

Maxim No. (*He puts the rose on the piano and plays again*)

Mrs de Winter comes further down the stairs

(*Stopping*) I don't seem to have seen you — since this morning.

Mrs de Winter You've been so busy, with the ship going ashore.

Maxim Yes. I was damnably ill-tempered this morning. I'm sorry.

Mrs de Winter It was my fault.

Maxim No, no, mine ... This affair tonight ... it's all rather an effort. I suddenly got fed up with the buffet tables in the dining-room and coils of wire on the terrace and idiotic little chairs dotted about the rose garden. And then that damn sea-fog on top of it all — liver, I suppose. Oh well, it'll be over in a few hours.

Mrs de Winter Manderley is looking lovely tonight. You'd think the house knew there was going to be a party. The moon's come out now the fog has lifted. Give me the rose.

Maxim (*picking up the rose*) What do you want it for?

Mrs de Winter Never you mind. (*She takes the rose from him*)

Maxim You look like a little criminal. What are you up to?

Mrs de Winter You'll see soon.

Maxim You don't look a bit like yourself. Make-up too.

Mrs de Winter Just a little.

Maxim You look different suddenly, as though ...

Mrs de Winter As though what?

Maxim I don't know. You had an expression on your face I've never seen before.

Mrs de Winter How do you mean?

Maxim When I first met you in Monte Carlo there was a look in your eyes. I can't define it. But it was one of the reasons I asked you to marry me. But just now ... something else was there instead.

Mrs de Winter What was there instead?

Maxim (*staring at her, then smiling*) You don't know what I'm talking about, do you? You're going to enjoy the party, aren't you, and dance every dance?

Mrs de Winter Will you dance with me?

Maxim My dancing days are over.

Mrs de Winter Oh, Maxim! Why, Beatrice told me you were a marvellous dancer.

Maxim I'm afraid she was pulling your leg.

Mrs de Winter looks away

What are you thinking about?

Mrs de Winter Why should I tell you? You never tell me what you are thinking.

Maxim You don't often ask me, do you?

Mrs de Winter I do, sometimes.

Maxim I don't remember.

Mrs de Winter I asked you the other day, in the library. You were standing looking out of the window.

Maxim Very probably. What did I say?

Mrs de Winter You told me you were wondering whether Surrey had beaten Middlesex.

Maxim (*laughing*) What a disappointment to you! What did you hope I was thinking?

Mrs de Winter Something very different.

Maxim What sort of thing?

Mrs de Winter Oh, I don't know.

Maxim I don't believe you do. If I told you I was thinking about Surrey and Middlesex, I was thinking about Surrey and Middlesex. Men are simpler than you imagine, my sweet child. Run along and get ready. The first cars will soon be here. What's it to be? Alice in Wonderland or the White Rabbit?

Mrs de Winter You'll get the surprise of your life when you do see me. I warn you now. The surprise of your life.

Maxim I'm sure I shall. I can hardly bear to wait.

The front doorbell rings; then there is the noise of voices and laughter

Go on, quick, there's somebody coming!

Mrs de Winter runs upstairs and exits

Frith enters c

Frith Major and Mrs Lacy.

Beatrice and Giles enter C. *Beatrice is dressed as an Eastern lady, Giles as an Arab*

Frith exits C

Maxim Oh! My Lord!
Beatrice Now don't start criticizing before you've even looked at us. They're the genuine thing, and belong to a friend of Giles's who's just come back from the East.
Maxim Pity he didn't stay out there! Your veil's crooked, old girl.
Beatrice What! Oh! Damn the thing. I've fixed it twenty times this evening. Has anyone got a pin?
Maxim I shouldn't think so. Giles, hadn't you better have a drink? You look like death already.
Giles I told Bee we'd much better come as a pierrot and pierrette, but she wouldn't hear of it.
Beatrice I'm sick of putting flour on my face, and a dunce's cap on my head.

Frank enters C

Frank (*seeing Beatrice and Giles*) I say ... You both look terrific! My congratulations!
Beatrice Maxim has been very offensive already. But I assure you, Frank, they're genuine, straight from the East.
Frank Really?
Maxim That's why they're so damn funny. Get Giles a drink, Frank. I think he's going to be sick.
Frank (*laughing and calling through the double doors*) Frith! Frith!

Frith enters C

A glass of champagne for Major Lacy.
Frith Yes, sir.
Beatrice Bring one for me too, Frith!
Frith Very good, madam.

Frith exits C

Maxim What have you got on underneath, old boy?
Giles A pair of old running drawers.
Beatrice They were the only things he could bear next to his skin. That's the

worst of that blanket material. Giles's friend warned us that it can give one prickly-heat eventually.

Giles Eventually, my foot! The thing's a blasted furnace already.

Maxim Well, you've got to keep it on now. I can't have you stripping here.

Giles I don't propose to strip ... Besides, it's not that sort of party.

Maxim You don't know what will be happening at five a.m.!

Frith enters with the glasses of champagne on a tray

Beatrice, Giles and Frank take a glass each

Come on, Giles, drown your sorrows. What on earth's that thing on your forehead, Bee?

Beatrice A virginity disc.

Maxim and Frank shout with laughter. Frith is quite overcome

Maxim Now you've made Frith spill the champagne.

Frith puts the tray on the table and exits c

Beatrice I think you're being very unkind, Maxim. The fact is, you're too idle to dress up yourself, and to save your face you have to jeer at us. I think the host ought to give the lead himself.

Maxim Heaven forbid!

Giles What are you supposed to be, Crawley?

Frank I'm afraid I left everything to the last moment ... so I thought I'd be a pirate. (*He pulls an eye-patch from his pocket*)

Giles Oh, good show. Where's our charming hostess?

Maxim Still dressing. I don't know what she's putting on. It's a terrific secret, and she hasn't told a soul. You don't know, do you, Frank?

Frank No, rather not.

Maxim She's like a little girl at her first party. Told me she was going to give us the surprise of our lives.

Beatrice My dear. How very exciting! Well, well, you don't seem to have forgotten many details, do you? I suppose the ballroom's looking marvellous. Has the band arrived?

Maxim They've been drinking beer heavily for the last half hour.

Giles Are Mitchell's doing the catering as usual?

Frank Yes, same old firm. Same familiar faces behind the buffet.

Maxim Same smoked salmon, and chickens' breasts in aspic.

Giles Same Perrier Jouet — nineteen twenty-one. (*He finishes his glass*) That's done me a power of good. I feel more like a sheikh than I did.

Beatrice I say, what's all this about a steamer going ashore?

Maxim Haven't you heard? Great excitement.

Beatrice Where is she?

Frank Between the beach and the headland. You know how that ridge runs out under the water? She went right on to it, but no casualties.

Giles Good Lord, what a mix-up!

Beatrice The trippers at Kerrith will be delighted. A wreck and the Manderley Ball on the same day. Can't you think of something else to give them? These excitements always run in threes.

Frank Don't say that, Mrs Lacy.

Maxim (*patting Frank on the shoulder*) We'll make Giles the third excitement. Midnight entrance without his blanket. (*He moves to the piano and begins to play*)

Beatrice This is always rather a frightful moment, isn't it, just before the thing begins. It's impossible to imagine that any moment the ballroom will be chock-a-block with people and there won't be room in there to move. Remember when I came as Madame Pompadour?

Giles Yes, and you tripped going into supper and your wig fell off! "I can't stand this damn thing", you said and chucked it into an ice-bucket.

Frank (*glancing at his watch*) Well, it's ten o'clock. The first car will be here any moment now.

Beatrice I say, that child of yours is going to be late.

Maxim I can't think what she's doing. She went up to dress hours ago.

There is the sound of a car approaching

Beatrice I believe there's the first car.

Headlights shine through the french windows

Frank (*going on to the terrace*) Yes, coming round the bend now ...

Maxim continues to play

Mrs de Winter comes through the archway to the head of the stairs. She is in the white dress, her hair is curled in ringlets, there is a white rose behind her ear

Mrs de Winter (*putting one hand on the banister*) How do you do, Mr de Winter.

Maxim stops playing the piano and stares up at Mrs de Winter

Maxim What the hell do you think you're doing?
Mrs de Winter What is it? What have I done?
Maxim Go and change. It doesn't matter what you put on. Find an ordinary
  evening frock, anything will do. Go now, before they see you. (*Harshly*)
  What are you standing there for? Didn't you hear what I said?
Beatrice Maxim ...

Mrs de Winter runs off

The sounds of more cars arriving are heard and the band strikes up as ——

—the Curtain *falls*

ACT II

Scene 1

The next morning. 4.30 a.m.

The hall is in semi-darkness. The last bars of a waltz are heard coming from the ballroom

Maxim comes down the stairs wearing an overcoat and exits through the french windows. Beatrice comes in c. *The telephone rings, and Beatrice moves to it*

Beatrice (*on the telephone*) Hallo, hallo. ... Has Mr de Winter left yet?... What on earth do you mean?

The band plays "God Save the King"

One moment ... (*She puts down the phone, shuts the double doors and returns*) Hallo, who is it? Hallo ... (*She pauses, then clicks the receiver*) Is that the Exchange? ... Somebody was trying to get on to us. ... No, they've rung off.

There is a pause

Giles enters c

Oh! Well leave it, then. ... Good-night. (*She replaces the receiver*)
Giles Who's ringing up at this unearthly hour? (*He switches on some lights*)
Beatrice I don't know. They rang off, whoever it was. I don't know what it was about. Lord, what a sight I look!
Giles What about it, Bee? Don't you think honour is satisfied? Let's slip away with the rest of the crowd. No-one will notice.
Beatrice Do you think we could? After all, the Ball has been a terrific success. Nobody has an inkling.
Giles Poor kid, she looked dead beat just now. God knows how she got through the evening.
Beatrice If only Maxim had given her one look, one smile!

Giles Why on earth did she do it? Where did she get hold of the dress? Of course Maxim thinks she did it on purpose.
Beatrice It's absurd to imagine for a moment that she did it deliberately.

Frank enters C

Frank Where's Maxim?
Beatrice Isn't he in the ballroom?
Frank The Lord Lieutenant is just going and wants to say good-night. Maxim's disappeared.

There is the noise of cars departing

Beatrice That's funny. Someone just telephoned to ask if he'd left.
Frank Who did?
Beatrice I don't know. They rang off. Oh, what does it matter? Frank, for heaven's sake go and say goodbye to the Trevelyans.

Frank moves to the double doors

Mrs de Winter enters through the double doors. She looks very white and very tired. She is dressed quite simply in a blue evening frock

Frank stops

(*To Mrs de Winter*) Hadn't you better go to bed? You look worn out.

Frank exits C

Giles Why not have a spot of brandy? It's only Dutch courage, but it sometimes works wonders.
Mrs de Winter No ... no, thank you.

Beatrice jerks her head at Giles to go away

Giles exits C

Beatrice You look awfully pale. Are you sure you're all right?
Mrs de Winter It's the morning light.
Beatrice It's ... been a big success. And you looked charming. Everyone said so. (*She pauses*) There's nothing to worry about. No-one knew anything about the ... the other thing. (*She pauses*) You understand, don't you, why it was such a shock to us when we saw you up there? That dress of my

grandmother's that you were wearing was ... was what Rebecca wore two years ago, at the same Midsummer party. You stood there and for one ghastly moment I thought ... You poor child! How were you to know?

Mrs de Winter I ought to have known ... I ought to have known ...

Beatrice Nonsense, how could you? It didn't make the slightest difference to the evening. We told people that your dress never turned up. It was perfectly natural.

Mrs de Winter What does it matter about the dress? I'm not thinking about the dress. I'm thinking of Maxim. What it's done to him.

Beatrice Don't you worry. Everything will be all right. I wish you'd go up to bed. Take a couple of aspirins and forget all about it. You'll feel so different when you've had a good long sleep.

Giles and Frank enter C. *Frank has his overcoat on*

Giles We can't find Maxim anywhere. Frank's been across to the car park. I don't know what old Trevelyan thought.

Beatrice What an extraordinary thing! Where can he have got to?

Frank He ... he may have gone for a walk.

Beatrice My dear, shall I come up with you and sit until Maxim comes back?

Mrs de Winter No, I'm all right.

Giles Come on, Bee. We're being a damn nuisance. Don't you worry now, Maxim will turn up directly. And that's a jolly pretty frock you're wearing; made the rest of us look damn silly.

Beatrice Good-night, my dear. (*She kisses Mrs de Winter*) Tell Maxim we had to go, and apologize for us. Say we had a wonderful evening, and that we know everyone enjoyed themselves enormously.

Frank Yes, of course I will.

Giles Good-night, Crawley.

Frank Good-night.

Giles and Beatrice exit C

Mrs de Winter Frank ——

Frank Yes?

Mrs de Winter Where *has* Maxim gone?

Frank I don't know.

Mrs de Winter I've got to see him. I've got to explain about tonight. Maxim thinks I did it on purpose.

Frank No.

Mrs de Winter He does, I tell you ... you didn't stand beside him all the evening watching him, as I did. He never spoke to me, he never looked at me once.

Frank There was no chance, with all those people. Of course I saw.

Mrs de Winter I'm not blaming him. I should have realized when I married Maxim that this had to happen. There was something I suspected and I tried to pretend to myself that it wasn't true.

Frank (*sharply*) What did you suspect?

Mrs de Winter About him and Rebecca.

Frank What do you mean?

Mrs de Winter He doesn't love me, he loves Rebecca. He thinks about her still, day and night. He's never loved me, Frank. It's always Rebecca, Rebecca ... Rebecca ...

Frank Look here, I've got to explain. You must listen to me — you must.

Mrs de Winter No, no. I don't want to go over and over it again. It's happened, it can't be altered now.

Frank But you don't see. You must let me talk to you.

Mrs de Winter Supposing he doesn't come back? Supposing he's gone away for ever?

Frank Of course he'll come back. Mrs de Winter, please ——

Mrs de Winter Don't call me that ——

Frank If you won't listen to me, you must listen to Maxim. I'm going to find him.

Frank exits through the french windows

Mrs de Winter breaks down and sits on the staircase

Mrs Danvers enters through the archway and stops on the landing

Mrs de Winter (*seeing Mrs Danvers*) You've done what you wanted. You meant this to happen, didn't you? Why do you hate me? What have I ever done to you that you should hate me?

Mrs Danvers You tried to take Mrs de Winter's place.

Mrs de Winter (*going up the stairs*) I love him, you don't seem to realize that. Haven't we as much right to be happy as anyone else?

Mrs Danvers Mr de Winter isn't happy; any fool can see that. He's in hell, and he's looked like that ever since she died.

Mrs de Winter That's not true. He was happy when we were in France together, he was younger, much younger, and laughing and happy.

Mrs Danvers Well, he's a man, isn't he? No man denies himself on his honeymoon. (*She turns to leave*)

Mrs de Winter How dare you speak to me like that? How dare you! (*She grabs Mrs Danvers by the arm*) You made me wear that dress, you did it because you wanted to hurt him. Hadn't he suffered enough without your playing that hideous trick on him?

Mrs Danvers What do I care for his suffering? He's never cared about mine. How does he think I've felt, watching you sit in her place, touching her things? What does he think it's meant to me knowing that you wrote at her desk in the morning-room, using the very pen she used? How does he think I've liked hearing Frith and Robert and the rest of the servants talking about you as Mrs de Winter? And all the while my lady lying cold and forgotten in the church crypt. If he suffers he deserves to suffer, marrying a girl like you not twelve months afterwards. Well, he's paying for it now, isn't he? I've seen his face. He knows she sees him. He knows she comes by night and watches him. And she doesn't come kindly, not she, not my lady. She was never one to stand by and be wronged. "I'll see them in hell first, Danny," she'd say. She did what she liked, she lived as she liked. She cared for nothing and for no-one.

Mrs de Winter What's the use of all this?

Mrs Danvers I remember her at sixteen on one of her father's horses, a big brute of an animal, too, that the groom said was too hot for her. She stuck to him, all right, slashing at him, drawing blood, digging the spurs in his side, and when she got off his back, he was trembling all over. "That'll teach him, won't it, Danny?" she said, and walked off to wash her hands as cool as you please. And that's how she went at life when she grew up. I saw her, I was with her. She cared for nothing and for no-one.

Mrs de Winter Mrs Danvers, you're not well, you ought to rest. You ought to go to your room and rest.

Mrs Danvers (*mimicking*) Go to my room, go to my room and rest. The mistress of the house thinks I'd better go to my room. And after that, what then? You'll go running to Mr de Winter and saying: "Mrs Danvers has been unkind to me. Mrs Danvers has been rude to me", as you did about Mr Favell yesterday!

Mrs de Winter I never said a word to him.

Mrs Danvers That's a lie. Who else told him if you didn't? Why shouldn't I see Mr Jack here at Manderley? He is the one link I have left now with my lady. Mr de Winter has not forgotten to be jealous, has he? He was jealous while she lived, and he's jealous now she's dead. So was everyone who knew her. A man had only to look at her once and be mad about her.

Mrs de Winter I don't want to know. I don't want to hear.

Mrs Danvers It's no use, is it? You'll never get the better of her. She's still the mistress here, even if she is dead. It's you that's the shadow, and the ghost. It's you that's unwanted and forgotten and pushed aside. Well, why don't you leave Manderley to her, why don't you go? (*She moves close to Mrs de Winter*)

Mrs de Winter slowly backs against the rail of the landing

He doesn't want you. He wants to be alone in the house again, with her. What's the use of your staying at Manderley? You're not happy, he doesn't love you. There's not much for you to live for, is there? Look down. It's easy. It's quick, kind, not like drowning. Why don't you fall? Why don't you? Let yourself go, there's nothing to be afraid of.

The telephone rings

Mrs Danvers exits through the archway

Frank enters through the french windows. He goes quickly to the telephone and picks up the receiver

Frank (*into the telephone*) Hallo ... hallo, yes, this is Mr Crawley speaking. What do you want? ... Inspector Welch. Yes!

Mrs de Winter (*descending the stairs*) Frank, something's happened to Maxim?

Frank (*into the telephone*) Where? When? How long ago? ... Yes. I understand ...

Mrs de Winter What is it? Have they found him?

Frank (*into the telephone*) He's just left you. He's on his way? ... Yes.

Mrs de Winter Is he all right?

Frank (*into the telephone*) Yes, of course, it's a ... a very serious matter.

Mrs de Winter What is it? What is it?

Frank (*into the telephone*) All right, Inspector. Thank you very much. Goodnight. (*He replaces the receiver*)

Mrs de Winter Tell me, Frank.

Frank It's all right. Maxim's quite safe. There's been no accident. He's on his way home now.

Mrs de Winter Oh, thank God! What's happened?

Frank He's been with Inspector Welch and Searle, the harbourmaster. They must have sent for him, and he slipped away without telling anyone.

Mrs de Winter Why should they send for him?

Frank That ship that went ashore ... the harbourmaster had to send a diver down to examine the keel. When the diver was below ... he found something else.

Mrs de Winter Go on, Frank, please ...

Frank A few yards away from the ship he found the hull of a sailing-boat.

Mrs de Winter Yes?

Frank It was the boat Rebecca was sailing when she was drowned. The hull was quite intact. The man looked in through the porthole, and he saw a body in the cabin.

Mrs de Winter A body?

Frank The harbourmaster told the police ... and they had to tell Maxim.

Mrs de Winter Frank, if there was a body there, it means that Rebecca was not alone when she was sailing.

Frank It looks like it.

Mrs de Winter Surely, if someone was missing, that would have been discovered before now. Who could it have been?

Frank I don't know. That's what the police have to find out. That's why they had to tell Maxim tonight.

Maxim enters through the french windows

Maxim Did the Inspector get hold of you?

Frank Yes.

Maxim He told you what had happened?

Frank Yes.

Maxim The diver is going down again later this morning. They'll try and raise the boat. I must be there.

Frank Is there anything you want me to do?

Maxim No.

Frank You'd better try and get some rest. I'll go home and change. Then I'll meet you down there.

Maxim Right!

Frank exits C

Mrs de Winter I'm so sorry. So terribly sorry. You've forgiven me, haven't you?

Maxim Forgiven you? What have I got to forgive you for?

Mrs de Winter Tonight. You thought I did it on purpose.

Maxim Oh, that ... I'd forgotten. I was angry with you, wasn't I?

Mrs de Winter Maxim, can't we start again? Face things together? I don't ask you to love me. But I don't want you to bear this alone.

Maxim No, it's too late. It's all over now. The thing has happened. The thing I've always foreseen. The thing I've dreamt about night after night.

Mrs de Winter What thing, Maxim?

Maxim Rebecca has won. She knew she would win, in the end.

Mrs de Winter Maxim, what do you mean?

Maxim Her boat. They've found it. The diver found it.

Mrs de Winter Yes, I know. Frank told me. You're thinking about the body in the cabin, aren't you?

Maxim Yes.

Mrs de Winter It means she was not alone. There was someone with her.

Maxim No. There was no-one with Rebecca, she was alone. There was no accident. Rebecca was not drowned. I killed her. I shot her down there in the cottage on the beach. I carried her body to the cabin, and took the boat out that night and sank it where they found it yesterday. It's Rebecca lying there on the cabin floor. (*He pauses*) You see, I was right. It's too late.

Mrs de Winter Does anyone else know about this?

Maxim No, no-one but you and me.

Mrs de Winter Frank ... Are you sure Frank does not know?

Maxim How could he know? There was nobody there that night except myself. I thought I should go mad, sitting here, day after day, answering all those terrible letters of sympathy. Then — that body was found at Salcombe and I took a chance. I went up and saw it. I said it was Rebecca's.

Mrs de Winter Why didn't you tell me?

Maxim How could I tell you? I wanted to blot out the past. I thought you could help me. But since we came home, you've been different.

Mrs de Winter Before we came to Manderley you were different too. Now I know you love Rebecca still.

Maxim What?

Mrs de Winter Every time you touch me I feel you're thinking of Rebecca.

Maxim Oh, my God!

Mrs de Winter It's true, isn't it?

Maxim You think I loved Rebecca? You think I killed her, loving her? I hated her. She was cold, vicious, rotten. We never loved each other, never had one moment of happiness together. Rebecca was incapable of love! But she was clever. My God, she was clever. No-one would guess meeting her that she was not the kindest, most generous, gifted person. When I married her, people told me I was the luckiest man in the world. I found her out, five days after we were married. She told me about herself, told me things I still could never repeat to a living soul! The luckiest man in the world! You despise me, don't you?

Mrs de Winter No ...

Maxim I don't want to tell you about those years. The filth, lies and deceit. I never gave her away. What she did in London did not touch me, because it did not touch Manderley. And she was careful the first few years. Then little by little she began to ask her friends down here if I were away. I warned her. I told her she could do what she liked in London, but Manderley was mine. She smiled, she didn't say anything. She began on poor Frank. He came to me one day, said he wanted to leave. I argued with him. He broke down and told me. She was always going down to his house, trying to get him ... to make love to her, and Frank was not the only one, there were others ... I began to be afraid she would get hold of anyone ... one of the workers on the estate, anyone ... and then the crash would come. She had a cousin, a fellow called Jack Favell. He began to come here when I was away. He had a filthy reputation. The very thought of him walking about here in Manderley made me mad. And at last I couldn't stand it any longer. One night I thought I should find Favell with her at the cottage. But she was alone. She was lying on the divan there, with an ashtray full of cigarette stubs beside her. She was smiling ... I told her that I would divorce her. She said had I thought how impossible it would be for me to make a case against her? Did I realize I hadn't one shred of proof? All our friends, even the servants, believed our marriage to be a success. Nobody would believe my story, nobody at all. And then ... then I remember she got up from the divan and stood in front of me, smoking a cigarette. "I haven't told Jack yet," she said. "I saw a doctor in London today. I am going to have a child, neither you nor anyone in the world will ever be able to prove that it isn't yours. It will grow up at Manderley, bearing your name. And you'll have to live here and watch Jack's child growing up at Manderley, playing in the garden, running in the woods. I'll be the perfect mother, as I've been the perfect wife. And nobody will ever guess, nobody will ever know." When I shot her she was smiling still ... I carried her out to the boat. It was very dark. There was no moon, I laid her in the cabin. I got the boat under way. I thought "I'll sink it in deep water beyond the headland", but the sail broke loose in the wind, and I was forced back towards the rocks. God, the water there would be too shallow! I found a spike, I drove it into the planks and the bottom boards, I jammed the cabin door, took to the dinghy ... The boat went down like a stone ... The wind suddenly dropped, it started raining. I rowed back to the shore. (*He pauses*) That's all. Rebecca has won. Finding you hasn't made any difference. It's too late.

Mrs de Winter It's not too late. I love you. Look at me, Maxim. You've got to believe me. Rebecca is dead. That's what we've got to remember. She can't speak, she can't bear witness. She can't harm you any more.

Maxim They'll identify the body. There's everything to tell them there in the cabin. The clothes she was wearing, the shoes, her jewellery.

Mrs de Winter If they find out it's Rebecca, you must say that when you went to Salcombe you made a mistake. You were confused. You were ill. You will say that, won't you?

Maxim does not answer

They can't prove anything against you. Nobody saw you that night. Nobody knows but you and I. We are the only two people in the world to know, you and I. They will think that the boat capsized and sank when she was in the cabin. They'll think Rebecca went below, and while she was there the wind came from the headland, and the boat capsized and Rebecca was trapped. They'll think that, won't they? Won't they?

The telephone begins to ring

Mrs de Winter puts her arms around Maxim

The CURTAIN *falls*

SCENE 2

About two o'clock in the afternoon — the same day

The hall is clear of decorations and flowers

As the CURTAIN *rises the telephone is ringing. Frith enters by the single door and answers it*

Frith (*into the telephone*) Manderley. ... No. Mr de Winter is not here ... I couldn't say. My orders are to give no statement whatsoever to the Press.

Mrs de Winter enters C

I can't help that. No, I have no information to give. (*He replaces the receiver*)
Mrs de Winter What did they want, Frith?
Frith The Press again, madam. The *County Chronicle* this time. They all asked the same question.
Mrs de Winter What is that?
Frith Whether it has been confirmed that the body in the boat is the late Mrs de Winter herself. If it's true, we shall all be very much distressed.
Mrs de Winter Yes ... I know.

Robert appears at the double doors

Frith Excuse me, madam. (*He moves to Robert*)

Robert whispers to Frith, then exits C

Mrs de Winter Yes, Frith?
Frith Robert tells me that Mr de Winter and Mr Crawley have left the mortuary and are on their way to the house now. They have Colonel Julyan with them.
Mrs de Winter Colonel Julyan?
Frith Yes, madam. He went to the mortuary with Mr de Winter, it seems, also Dr Phillips and Inspector Welch. It can't be very pleasant for Mr de Winter, to have the police concerned in the matter.
Mrs de Winter No.
Frith Do you feel unwell, madam? Shall I call Alice?
Mrs de Winter No — no, I'm all right. It's very hot here.
Frith Yes, madam. Very warm indeed.

Maxim enters C

Maxim Colonel Julyan and Mr Crawley are outside.
Frith Yes, sir.

Frith exits C

Mrs de Winter What ... what happened?
Maxim (*quickly*) Phillips identified the body himself, almost at once. It was
straightforward, simple. There was no trace of what I'd done. The bullet
hadn't touched the bone.
Mrs de Winter Is it ... going to be all right?
Maxim I think so — I can't be certain yet. They think she was trapped in the
cabin. There's no alternative but that. There's no evidence of anything else.
Mrs de Winter Are you sure?

Frith enters C, *showing in Colonel Julyan and Frank. Frith exits* C

Colonel Julyan How do you do. I little thought at your party that we should
meet again so soon.
Mrs de Winter No.
Colonel Julyan This is a very distressing and unfortunate occurrence. I do
feel for you and your husband most acutely.
Mrs de Winter Thank you.
Colonel Julyan What makes it so awkward is the fact that your husband
identified that other body nearly a year ago.
Mrs de Winter Yes, I realize that.
Frank I think the mistake was very natural under the circumstances. The
authorities wrote to Maxim, asking him to go up to Salcombe presupposing
before he arrived there that the body was Mrs de Winter's. And Maxim was
not well at the time.
Maxim That's nonsense. I was perfectly well.
Colonel Julyan Well, it's no use going into that now. You made the first
identification, and now the only thing to do is to admit the error. There
seems to be no doubt about it this time.
Maxim No.
Colonel Julyan I wish you could be spared the publicity of an inquest, but
that is impossible.
Mrs de Winter When will the inquest be?
Maxim Day after tomorrow.
Colonel Julyan The only consolation is that now we know that your late
wife's death must have been swift and sudden, not the dreadful lingering
affair we all believed it to be. There's no question now of her having tried
to swim ashore.
Maxim No.

Colonel Julyan She must have gone below for something, and then the door jammed, and a squall caught the boat with no-one at the helm.

Maxim Yes.

Colonel Julyan That seems to be the solution, don't you think so, Crawley?

Frank Oh yes! Undoubtedly.

Colonel Julyan I suppose sooner or later we all make an error in judgment, and then we are for it.

Maxim Yes, I suppose so.

Colonel Julyan She ought to have known how treacherous the wind can be just there, and that it wasn't safe to leave the helm.

Frank It was very squally that night, something may have happened to the gear.

Colonel Julyan Well, we shall never know now.

Frith enters c

Frith Excuse me, sir. But William Tabb is here. He said he was asked to call.

Colonel Julyan That's quite right. I told him to come up. I hope you don't mind, de Winter, but I thought it would be a good idea to find out from him before the inquest if your wife's boat was seaworthy, and in good order when it was last in his yard. I hope you don't mind.

Maxim Of course not. It's very kind of you to take so much trouble. Show him in, Frith.

Frith Yes, sir.

Frith exits

Mrs de Winter offers cigarettes to Colonel Julyan

Colonel Julyan No, thank you! Most unfortunate this affair should happen almost simultaneously with your party. Everyone enjoyed it so much.

Mrs de Winter Thank you.

Colonel Julyan Does an immense amount of good locally, that sort of thing.

Maxim I'm glad you think so.

Frith enters with Tabb, c

Frith Here is Mr Tabb, sir.

Frith exits

Maxim Good-afternoon, Tabb. I think Colonel Julyan wants to ask you a few questions.

Tabb Yes, sir.

Frank Good-day, William.

Tabb Good-day, sir.

Colonel Julyan Oh, Tabb! We just wanted to make sure about one or two things that have been bothering us. You know, I suppose, that the late Mrs de Winter's boat has been found?

Tabb Yes, sir.

Colonel Julyan You used to do the boat up every year, didn't you?

Tabb Yes, sir.

Colonel Julyan What we want to know is whether or not that boat was in a fit state to put to sea.

Tabb She was, when I fitted her out in April last year.

Colonel Julyan Was she a difficult boat to handle?

Tabb Everyone has to have their wits about them when they go sailing boats, I don't deny it, sir. But she was a stout, seaworthy boat, and Mrs de Winter had sailed her in worse weather than she ever found that night. That's what I've said all along. I couldn't understand the boat being lost on a night like that.

Colonel Julyan I was away at the time, so I can't give an opinion. Would you say it blew very hard that night, de Winter?

Maxim No, not particularly — I don't think so. Fits and starts.

Frank It was blowing quite hard from my house. Maxim wouldn't notice it so much here at Manderley.

Colonel Julyan (*to Maxim*) Do you agree with Tabb that the boat would stand a lot of wind?

Maxim Yes, I should have thought so.

Tabb She'd stand any amount of wind, sir; she was a fishing boat before I converted her. Those boats will stand almost anything.

Colonel Julyan But if Mrs de Winter went below for a coat, as we imagine, and a sudden gust of wind came from the headland, that would have been enough to capsize the boat, wouldn't it?

Tabb No, I don't see that it would.

Colonel Julyan I'm afraid that's what must have happened all the same. Well, Tabb, that's all we wanted to know. We don't blame you in any way, you know.

Tabb Excuse me, sir, but there's a little more to it than that.

Colonel Julyan Well?

Tabb It's like this, sir. After the accident last year a lot of people made unpleasantness about my work. Some said I had let Mrs de Winter start the season in a leaky, rotten boat. I lost two or three customers because of it. It was very unfair, but the boat had gone, and there was nothing I could say to clear myself. Then this morning when Mrs de Winter's boat was brought to the surface, the harbourmaster gave me permission to look at her, and I did. I wanted to satisfy myself that the work I had put into her was sound,

in spite of the fact that she's been lying water-logged these twelve months.
Colonel Julyan Well, that was very natural. I hope you were satisfied.
Tabb Yes, sir. I was. There was nothing wrong with that boat as regard the
work I did to her. I examined every corner of her.
Colonel Julyan Good!
Tabb What I want to know, sir, is this. Who drove the holes in her planking?
Rocks didn't do it.
Colonel Julyan What holes?
Tabb There were three of them. Done with a spike, I'd say. One right for'ard,
by her chain locker, on her starboard planking below the water-line. The
other two close together amidships, underneath her floor boards in the
bottom. And that's not all ...
Colonel Julyan Go on!
Tabb Both sea-cocks were fully open! It wouldn't have taken long for her
to sink, with those holes driven in her, and open sea-cocks, not more than
ten minutes, I should say. It's my opinion, sir, that the boat never capsized
at all. She was deliberately scuttled.
Colonel Julyan What! I say, de Winter, do you hear what Tabb says?
Maxim Yes, I hear.
Colonel Julyan Did you know anything of these ... holes in the planking?
Maxim Nothing whatsoever.
Frank William, you must have made a mistake.
Tabb No, sir. I'd swear it.
Colonel Julyan If that's the case, then I'm afraid the whole affair is not so
simple as we thought. All right, Tabb, thank you. We shall want you at the
inquest, of course. Have you anything to ask him, de Winter?
Maxim No. Tell Frith to give you a drink, Tabb.
Mrs de Winter I'll go.

Tabb and Mrs de Winter exit c

Colonel Julyan I gather this is something of a shock to you, de Winter?
Maxim Does it surprise you that I should be shocked?
Colonel Julyan Mr de Winter, please understand, I feel very much for you
over this. Of course it's a shock and I sympathize with you. I want to help
you and to find out for you just exactly what happened. I'm not here for my
own amusement!
Maxim That's rather obvious, isn't it?
Colonel Julyan I hope it is ... Do you doubt Tabb's word in any way?
Maxim No, of course not. He is a boat-builder. He knows what he's talking
about.
Colonel Julyan Who looked after Mrs de Winter's boat when she was
actually in commission?
Maxim She looked after it herself.

Colonel Julyan She didn't employ any crew?
Maxim No, nobody at all.
Colonel Julyan The boat was always kept moored in the same place?
Maxim Yes.
Colonel Julyan There isn't any public footpath to the beach, is there? Any
trespasser would be seen.
Maxim Yes.
Frank Not necessarily. It's very shut in down there. There are a lot of trees.
Colonel Julyan It's hardly likely that a stranger would have gone and
tampered with the boat, is it?
Maxim Very unlikely.
Colonel Julyan And Tabb said the boat could not have stayed afloat for more
than ten minutes, with those holes in her. If they were there before Mrs de
Winter went for her evening sail, the boat would have sunk at her moorings.
Maxim No doubt.

Mrs de Winter enters c

Colonel Julyan Therefore the holes must have been driven in, and the cocks
opened, when the boat was out in the bay?
Maxim I suppose so.
Colonel Julyan I'm afraid the whole thing has become ... rather serious, de
Winter. At the inquest you will be asked all sorts of painful, intimate
questions. I'm speaking to you as a friend now and not as an official. May
I ask you something very personal?
Maxim If you like.
Colonel Julyan Were relations between you and the late Mrs de Winter ...
perfectly happy?
Maxim I think ...

Mrs de Winter falls to the ground

(*Moving swiftly to his wife*) Get some brandy, Frank, will you?
Frank Yes. (*He moves to the drinks table*)
Colonel Julyan I'm most frightfully sorry. Is there anything I can do?
Maxim No. She'll be round in a minute. She's tired — she had very little
sleep last night.
Colonel Julyan Yes, of course. She must be extremely upset. I'm so sorry ...

Frank brings a glass of brandy. Mrs de Winter stirs and opens her eyes

Mrs de Winter Maxim.
Maxim It's all right. Drink this.

Mrs de Winter (*drinking a little*) I felt very ... hot, standing there.
Maxim Yes, I know. Don't worry.
Colonel Julyan I think perhaps we'd better go on with our talk somewhere else. I must apologize, I hadn't realized Mrs de Winter was unwell.
Maxim It's all right.
Colonel Julyan Would it be convenient, Crawley, if we went to your office?
Maxim Of course. Frank, take Colonel Julyan down and I'll follow you in a few minutes.
Frank Will you come with me then, sir?
Colonel Julyan Yes ... Yes ...

Frank and Colonel Julyan exit c

Maxim supports his wife to a couch

Maxim Better?
Mrs de Winter Yes ...
Maxim You heard what Tabb said about the boat. No-one will believe it an accident any more.
Mrs de Winter You mean they will think it was you?
Maxim I don't know.
Mrs de Winter Maxim, nobody knows about the child. Could that be discovered now, after all these months?
Maxim No, it's impossible.
Mrs de Winter Then, if they don't know the reason, why should they think it was you? How can they prove anything against you? If they ask you outright, you'll lie to them, won't you? Maxim, you'll lie to them?
Maxim I've got to go now. They're waiting for me.
Mrs de Winter If anything happens ... they will let us be together ... won't they?
Maxim I only mind for you. I don't regret anything else. If it had to happen all over again I shouldn't do anything different ... but I can't forget that funny, young, lost look that I loved gone in a few hours.

He leaves c

The CURTAIN *falls*

SCENE 3

Early evening. 26th June

As the CURTAIN *rises the doorbell rings twice*

Frith crosses the outer hall towards the front door. There is a murmur of voices, off

Mrs de Winter comes to the head of the stairs

In a moment Frith comes into the hall

Mrs de Winter Who is it, Frith?
Frith A gentleman called Mr Favell.
Mrs de Winter Mr Favell.
Frith Yes, madam. I think he's come from the inquest.
Mrs de Winter I'll see him.
Frith Very good, madam.

Frith exits C. *He returns with Favell*

Frith Mr Favell, madam.

Frith exits C

Mrs de Winter Maxim is not here. I don't know when he will be back. Wouldn't it be better if you made an appointment to see him at the office in the morning?
Favell Waiting doesn't worry me, and I don't think I shall have to wait very long, you know.
Mrs de Winter It's quite possible he won't be home at all this evening.
Favell He's run off, has he? Of course, under the circumstances that may be the wisest thing to do. Gossip is an unpleasant thing to some people, isn't it?
Mrs de Winter What do you want to see Maxim about?
Favell (*lighting a cigarette*) You don't mind my smoking, I suppose? It won't make you sick, will it? One never knows with brides. You've grown up a bit since I saw you last, haven't you? I wonder what you have been doing? Leading Frank Crawley up the garden path? (*He helps himself to a whisky and sits down*) Well, it's all over. They finished about ten minutes ago.

Mrs de Winter Finished?

Favell Yes. The result caused rather a stir.

Mrs de Winter What do you mean?

Favell Worried, eh? I don't blame you. I'd be worried if I were you. (*He pauses*) They took an age to reach a decision. The Coroner asked so many questions. Lots of little details about the boat. Was the cabin door firmly shut? Where exactly were those ... those holes in the planking. Could a woman make them? And why were the sea-cocks turned on? And then they went and consulted for an hour before giving their verdict. Would you like to know what it was?

Mrs de Winter Mr Favell, I don't want to be rude, but as a matter of fact I'm very tired. I've had a long and fairly exhausting day.

Favell No, no, don't be a brute. I've had an exhausting day too. I'm quite harmless, really I am. I suppose Max has been telling tales about me? You think I'm a big, bad wolf, but I'm not, you know. I'm a perfectly ordinary, harmless bloke. I take off my hat to you. I really do. You come down here to Manderley, you take on all this place, meet hundreds of people you've never seen before, you put up with old Max and his moods, you don't give a fig for anyone. I call it a damn good effort. (*He sways, steadies himself, and puts down his glass*) I'm sorry, I'm sorry. This business has been a shock to me, you know. Rebecca was my cousin. We were brought up together. Liked the same things, the same people. Laughed at the same jokes. I suppose I was fonder of Rebecca than anyone else in the world. And she was fond of me. All this has been a bloody shock.

Mrs de Winter Yes, of course.

Favell (*savagely*) The verdict was suicide — without sufficient evidence to show the state of mind of the deceased.

Mrs de Winter Suicide?

Favell Yes. You didn't expect that, did you?

Mrs de Winter I — I don't know. I hadn't thought ...

Favell No, of course you hadn't. You were thinking about a very different verdict. Suicide! That's a good joke, isn't it? That old fool of a Coroner got the jury to say suicide. You and I know it wasn't suicide, don't we? Don't we?

The double doors open and Maxim comes into the hall with Frank

Maxim What the hell are you doing here?

Favell As a matter of fact, Max, old chap, I've come to congratulate you on the result of the inquest.

Maxim Do you mind leaving the house? Or do you want me to throw you out?

Favell Steady a minute. You don't want the servants to hear what I'm going to say, do you? Well, they will, if you don't shut the doors.

Frank shuts the doors

You've come pretty well out of this affair, haven't you? Better than you
ever expected? It was touch and go; very lucky for you it went the way it
did. You hadn't squared those thick-headed fellows who were acting jury
by any chance, had you?

Maxim moves towards him, but Favell holds up his hand

Wait a bit, can't you? I haven't finished yet. You realize, don't you, that
I can make things damned unpleasant for you if I choose? Not only
unpleasant, but ... dangerous.

Maxim In what way?

Favell Look here, Max. I suppose there are no secrets between you and your
wife, and Crawley there makes just the happy trio. I can speak plainly. You
know Rebecca and I were lovers? Very well, then. I believed, like every
other fool, that Rebecca was drowned, and that her body was picked up at
Salcombe weeks afterwards. Then I read in the evening papers that
Rebecca's boat had been found by the local diver and there was a body in
the cabin. Who the hell would Rebecca have as a sailing companion? It
didn't make sense. I got in touch with Danny. She told me then that the body
in the cabin was Rebecca's. Well, I attended the inquest today. And
everything went smoothly, didn't it, until Tabb gave his evidence? But
after that? Well, Max, what have you got to say about those holes in the
planking, and those sea-cocks turned full on?

Maxim You heard the evidence, and you heard the verdict. It satisfied the
Coroner, and it must satisfy you.

Favell Suicide! Rebecca commit suicide! Very like her! Listen! (*He takes
a note from his pocket*) You never knew I had this note, did you? I kept it,
because it was the last thing she ever wrote to me. I think it will interest you.
She wrote it the day she died. (*He reads*) "I tried to ring you at the flat but
could get no answer. I'm going down to Manderley right away. I want you
to follow me down. I'll spend the night at the cottage and I'll leave the door
open. I've got something to tell you, and I want to see you as soon as
possible — Rebecca." (*He puts the note back in his pocket*) That's not the
sort of thing one writes before committing suicide, is it? As it happened,
I didn't find it in time. I was at a party that night. When I read the note at
four in the morning I decided it was too late to go crashing down a six-hour
run to Manderley. I went to bed, determined to put a call through later in
the day. I did. About twelve o'clock. And I heard Rebecca had been
drowned. (*He pauses*) Supposing the Coroner this afternoon had read that
note? It would have made it a little more tricky for you, wouldn't it, Max,
old man?

Maxim Well, why didn't you get up and give it to him?

Favell No need to get rattled. I don't want to smash you, Max. God knows you've never been a friend to me, but I don't bear malice about it. All married men with lovely wives are jealous, aren't they? And some of 'em just can't help playing Othello. I'm sorry for them. I'm a bit of a Socialist in my way, you know, and I can't think why fellows can't share their women instead of killing them. A lovely woman isn't like a motor tyre, she doesn't wear out. The more you use her, the better she goes. Now, Max, I've laid all my cards on the table. I'm not a rich man. I'm too fond of gambling for that. Now if I had a settlement of two or three thousand a year for life I could jog along quite comfortably. And I'd never trouble you again. I swear I wouldn't ...

Maxim I asked you before to leave my house; I'm not going to ask you again.

Frank Half a minute, Maxim, it's not quite so easy as all that. (*To Favell*) It happens, very unfortunately, that you could, as you say, twist things around and make it difficult for Maxim. I don't think he sees it as clearly as I do. What is the exact amount you propose Maxim should settle on you?

Maxim Don't interfere with this, Frank. I'm not going to give in to blackmail.

Favell I don't suppose your wife wants to be pointed out as Mrs de Winter, the widow of a murderer?

Maxim Colonel Julyan is outside in Mr Crawley's car. He'll be interested in your story. Shall I ask him to come in?

Favell (*laughing*) Good bluff, but it won't work. You wouldn't dare. Max, old man, I've got enough evidence in this note to hang you.

Maxim turns and heads towards the c doors

Mrs de Winter Stop him, Frank, stop him!

Maxim exits

Frank, can't you do something? Go and tell Colonel Julyan it's a mistake.

Frank moves to the doors

Maxim enters c, followed by Colonel Julyan

Colonel Julyan Good-evening. (*To Favell*) Your face seems familiar. I've seen you before somewhere.

Maxim Jack Favell. My late wife's cousin. All right, Favell, go ahead.

Favell Look here, Colonel Julyan, there's no sense in beating about the bush. I'm not satisfied with the verdict today.

Colonel Julyan Oh, isn't that for de Winter to say, not you?

Favell No, I don't think it is. I have a right to speak, not only as Rebecca's cousin, but as her prospective husband had she lived.

Colonel Julyan Oh, I see. Is this true, de Winter?

Maxim It's the first I've heard of it.

Colonel Julyan Well, Favell, what exactly is your trouble?

Favell (*showing the note to Colonel Julyan*) This was written a few hours before Rebecca was supposed to have set out on that suicidal trip. I want you to read it and say whether you think the woman who wrote that note had made up her mind to kill herself.

Colonel Julyan takes the note from Favell and reads it

Colonel Julyan No, on the face of it, no. But I have no idea what the note refers to. Your cousin says she had something to tell you. Do you know what it was?

Favell (*taking the note from Colonel Julyan*) My cousin made a definite appointment in that note. What it actually was that she wanted to tell me, I don't know, but that's beside the point. She was intending to spend the night at the cottage on purpose to see me. The mere fact of her going for a sail never surprised me. It was what she loved doing after a day in London. But to drive holes in the planking of her own boat, and deliberately drown herself — the hysterical impulse of a neurotic girl — oh, no, Colonel Julyan, by Christ, no!

Colonel Julyan My dear fellow, it's not the slightest use your shouting at me. I'm not the Coroner who conducted the inquest, nor am I a member of the jury who gave the verdict. Naturally I want to help you all I can, and de Winter, too. You say you refuse to believe your cousin committed suicide. Suppose we get to the point. What do you suggest happened?

Favell Rebecca never killed herself. You've asked for my opinion, and by God you shall have it. Rebecca was murdered. And if you want to know who the murderer is, why there he is, with that God-damned superior smile on his face. He couldn't even wait, could he, until the year was out, before marrying the first girl he set eyes on. There he is, there's your murderer for you. Mr Maximilian de Winter. Take a good long look at him. He'd look well hanging. (*He laughs*)

Colonel Julyan stares at him for a moment

Colonel Julyan The man's drunk. He doesn't know what he's saying.

Favell Don't I? Oh, no, my friend. You're a magistrate, aren't you, and a colonel into the bargain? That doesn't cut any ice with me. I've got the law on my side for a change, and I'm going to use it. There are other magistrates in this bloody country. Fellows with brains. Not broken down old soldiers who got the sack years ago for incompetence and walk about with a string of putty medals on their chest. Max de Winter murdered Rebecca and he's not going to get away with it.

Colonel Julyan Wait a minute, Mr Favell. You were present at the inquest this afternoon. I remember you now. I saw you sitting there. If you felt so deeply about the verdict why didn't you say so then, to the jury, to the Coroner himself. Why didn't you produce that letter in court?

Favell (*laughing*) Because I did not choose to, that's why. I preferred to come and tackle de Winter personally.

Maxim I asked him the same question. Why didn't he tell his suspicions to the Coroner? He said he was not a rich man, and that if I cared to settle two or three thousand on him for life he would never worry me again.

Frank It's perfectly true, sir. It's blackmail, pure and simple.

Colonel Julyan You have just made a serious accusation against de Winter. Have you any proof to back that accusation?

Favell Proof? Aren't the holes in the boat proof enough?

Colonel Julyan Certainly not. Unless you can bring witnesses who saw him do it. Where's your witness?

Favell Witness be damned! Of course de Winter did it. Who else would kill Rebecca?

Colonel Julyan Kerrith has a large population. Why not go from door to door making enquiries? I might have done it myself. You appear to have no more proof against de Winter than you have against me.

Favell Oh, I see, you're going to hold his hand through this, because you've dined with him. He's a big noise down here. He's the owner of Manderley. You little snob.

Colonel Julyan Be careful, Favell. You say you were going to marry your cousin had she lived, that you were her lover, that you had a secret meeting with her at the cottage. You can't prove that, can you?

Favell Can't I? (*He smiles, then moves and rings the bell*)

Colonel Julyan What are you doing?

Favell You'll see.

Frith enters C

Favell Tell Mrs Danvers to come here.

Frith glances at Maxim. Maxim looks as if he is about to speak but hesitates a fraction of a second

This won't be easy, will it, Max?

Maxim All right, Frith. We would like to see Mrs Danvers.

Frith Mrs Danvers went to the inquest, sir. I'm not sure whether she is back yet.

Maxim Go and see, will you?
Frith Yes, sir.

He exits C

Colonel Julyan Mrs Danvers is your housekeeper, isn't she, de Winter?
Maxim Yes.
Favell She was also my cousin's devoted friend. Danny will tell you the truth all right. That verdict of suicide will have been a shock to her. Almost as big a shock as it's been to me.

Mrs Danvers comes in C. *She is plainly dressed in a coat and hat*

Mrs Danvers You wish to see me, sir?
Maxim Colonel Julyan wants to ask you something, Mrs Danvers.
Colonel Julyan I have Mr de Winter's permission to ask you this question, Mrs Danvers. Were you aware of the relationship between Mr Favell here and the late Mrs de Winter? (*He pauses*) I was not referring to blood relationship, Mrs Danvers, I mean something closer than that.
Mrs Danvers I'm afraid I don't understand, sir.
Favell Oh, come off it, Danny. You know what he's driving at. I've told him already, but he won't believe me. Rebecca and I lived together on and off for years, didn't we? She was in love with me, wasn't she?
Mrs Danvers She was not.
Favell Don't be a fool, Danny ...
Mrs Danvers She was not in love with you or anyone. She despised you all.
Favell Listen here. Didn't she meet me at the cottage, night after night? Didn't we spend the weekends together in London?
Mrs Danvers Well, and what if she did? She had a right to amuse herself, hadn't she? Love-making was a game with her, only a game. She did it because it made her laugh. I've known her come back here and rock with laughter at the lot of you. (*She sits and slowly begins to cry*)
Colonel Julyan Favell, give me that note.

Favell hands the note to Colonel Julyan

We are trying to find the motive for Mrs de Winter's suicide. Mr Favell is not satisfied with the verdict. Can you think of any reason why she should have taken her own life?
Mrs Danvers No, I can't.
Colonel Julyan I want you to read this note which the late Mrs de Winter wrote to her cousin the morning of the day she died. Can you throw any light on it?

Mrs Danvers takes the note and reads it

Mrs Danvers I've no idea what she means. If there was something important she had to tell Mr Jack, she would have told me first.

Colonel Julyan (*taking the note back*) You never saw her that night?

Mrs Danvers No, I was out. I shall never forgive myself for that. Never, till my dying day.

Colonel Julyan Those words, "I have something to tell you", convey nothing to you at all?

Mrs Danvers No, nothing at all.

Colonel Julyan If we knew what she meant by those words, "I have something to tell you", we would have the answer to the whole problem. In those words can lie the motive for suicide or murder.

Maxim I agree with you. Very well then. What are we going to do? How can any of us discover what she meant by those words now?

Colonel Julyan Does anyone know how she spent that last day in London?

Mrs Danvers I have a diary belonging to the late Mrs de Winter. If you think it will be helpful I will go and fetch it.

Colonel Julyan What do you say, de Winter? Do you mind my seeing this diary?

Maxim Of course not. Why should I?

Mrs Danvers exits c

Favell Playing for time, that's what you're doing, the whole damn lot of you. You're just like a trade union, aren't you? No-one is going to give away anything. Even the local magistrate is in the same racket. We must exempt the bride, of course. A wife doesn't give evidence against her husband. Crawley, of course, was squared long ago. He knew he'd lose his job if he told the truth. And if I guess rightly, Crawley, there's a spice of malice in you towards me. You didn't have much success with Rebecca, did you? The garden path was just a shade too long, eh, old boy? The bride will be grateful for your fraternal arm in a week or so. Frank will come in very handy, Max, when the judge sentences you to hang! (*He laughs*)

Maxim rushes at Favell. Frank pulls Maxim away

Colonel Julyan (*to Mrs de Winter*) I think you had better leave us.

Mrs de Winter No. I must stay.

Favell Oh God, I need a whisky! (*He gets to his feet and pours himself a whisky*)

Mrs Danvers enters c *with a diary*

Mrs Danvers Here it is, sir, here are all her appointments on the date she died.
(She gives the diary to Julyan)
Colonel Julyan *(putting on his spectacles and perusing the diary)* Here we
are. *(He reads)* "June the fourth. Hair — ten-thirty."
Mrs Danvers I remember that. I telephoned earlier in the week to book it for
her.
Colonel Julyan A cross beside it. What does that mean?
Mrs Danvers That means she kept the appointment.
Colonel Julyan I see. *(He reads)* "Twelve o'clock. Lunch at the club."
Rather early for lunch, wasn't it?
Mrs Danvers No, she always lunched early when she had her hair done.
Colonel Julyan *(reading)* "Two o'clock: Baker." Who was Baker?
Mrs Danvers She knew no-one with that name.
Colonel Julyan Well, here it is. And she's put a great cross beside the name
as if she wanted to break the pencil. She evidently kept the appointment.
You look, Crawley.
Mrs Danvers I have never heard the name before.
Favell The butcher, the baker, the candlestick maker. All jumped out of a
rotten potato.
Colonel Julyan Know of anyone of that name, de Winter?
Maxim No — not a soul.
Frank *(turning over the pages of the book)* Here's something — right at the
back among the telephone numbers. *(He reads)* "Baker. Something o-
four-double-four."
Colonel Julyan That's his number, all right, o-four-double-four, but I can't
make out the exchange at all.
Favell Try every exchange in London. It will take you through the night, but
we don't mind.
Mrs Danvers Let me look, sir.

Frank hands her the book

(Looking at the page) That's M-U.
Maxim Museum o-four-double-four.
Colonel Julyan You know that number, then?
Maxim No, but it's pretty obvious, isn't it?
Colonel Julyan Try that number, Crawley.
Maxim Go on, Frank. What are you waiting for?
Frank *(moving to the telephone and picking up the receiver)* Will you put
a call through to London Museum o-four-double-four? Thank you.
Colonel Julyan Mrs Danvers, had Mrs de Winter some enemy? Someone
she was afraid of?
Mrs Danvers She was afraid of nothing and of no-one. There was only one
thing that ever worried her and that was the idea of getting old and dying

in her bed. She said to me scores of times: "When I go, Danny, I want to go suddenly, like the snuffing out of a candle." That used to be the only thing that consoled me after she died. They told me drowning was painless.

Colonel Julyan I suppose she wasn't in the hands of moneylenders?

Mrs Danvers Mrs de Winter? Moneylenders?

Colonel Julyan Well, blackmailers, perhaps.

Favell What the hell's the use of all this? Who the hell cares about this Baker fellow? What's he got to do with it? It was probably some damn merchant who sold stockings or face-cream. If it had been anyone important, Danny here would know him. Rebecca had no secrets from Danny.

The telephone rings

Frank (*picking up the receiver: into the phone*) Thank you. Hallo! ... Is that Museum o-four-double-four? ... Can you tell me if anyone of the name Baker lives there? ... What address is it? ... Who is speaking? ... Mrs Baker? ... Yes, if you will, please. It's rather important. (*To the others*) I think we've got him. It's an address in Bloomsbury. A Dr Baker. He's coming to the telephone now. What do you want me to say?

Favell A doctor? What the hell did Rebecca want with a doctor?

Frank (*into the telephone*) Would you hold the line one minute, please?

Mrs Danvers I've never heard her speak of a Dr Baker. She never mentioned a doctor to me.

Frank Well? What am I to say?

Maxim Colonel Julyan?

Colonel Julyan Yes.

Maxim I think you had better speak to Dr Baker.

Colonel Julyan (*taking the receiver from Frank; into it*) Good-evening, Dr Baker. Would you please forgive a rather unorthodox call at such an hour! It is a matter of vital importance. My name is Julyan, Colonel Julyan. I'm a magistrate in Cornwall. I must explain, Dr Baker, that in an inquest held today on the body of a certain Mrs de Winter, the jury returned a verdict of suicide. Her relatives are not satisfied with that verdict. We believe that in June last year she had an appointment with you. I can give you the exact date. It was June the fourth at two o'clock. Would you be good enough to verify this. (*He puts his hand over the receiver; to Maxim*) You don't object if I ask why Mrs de Winter made that appointment?

Maxim No.

Colonel Julyan (*into the telephone again*) Ah, you've found it. I know it's not etiquette to ask but the circumstances are very unusual. Could you tell me why she consulted you that day? I feel her appointment with you must have had some bearing on the case and her subsequent ... suicide. ... Yes. ... Yes. ... Yes. ... Yes. ... I see. ... Yes. ... Thank you. I'll communicate with you officially in the morning. ... Could you hold on a moment? (*He covers the receiver; to the others*) Mrs de Winter first consulted him in May. He took some X-rays. When she went again on June the fourth, he showed her the photographs. She had cancer.

Maxim Cancer?

Colonel Julyan You had no idea?

Maxim No. No.

Colonel Julyan (*into the telephone*) Would you be kind enough to speak to Mr de Winter? (*He gives the telephone to Maxim*)

Maxim (*into the telephone*) Dr Baker? Good-evening. I'm Maxim de Winter. ... Yes. ... Could you ... ? (*He listens*) But she seemed perfectly healthy. ... I see. ... Yes. ... Yes. ... Thank you. (*He puts down the telephone*) Baker says that her pain was slight, but the growth was deep rooted, and in three or four months she would have been under morphia. An operation would have been of no use ... The X-rays also showed a malformation of the uterus which meant she could never have a child; but that was quite apart, it had nothing to do with the cancer.

Favell (*shaken*) Good God. Not the sort of thing you'd connect with Rebecca — cancer! Do you fellows feel like a drink? (*He pours himself a whisky*) I'm all out over this. Cancer! Oh, my God!

Colonel Julyan Pull yourself together, Favell.

Favell Oh, you're all right, you're fine. Max is on a good wicket now, isn't he? You've got your motive for suicide, and Baker will supply it in black and white free of cost, whenever you send the word. You can dine at Manderley once a week on the strength of it and feel proud of yourself. No doubt, Max will ask you to be godfather to his first child.

Colonel Julyan I would advise you to go straight back to your hotel or whatever and go to bed. I may as well warn you now, as I shall not be seeing you again, that blackmail is not much of a profession, Mr Favell. And we know how to deal with it in our part of the world, strange though it may seem to you.

Favell (*to Maxim*) Yes, it's been a stroke of luck for you, Maxim, hasn't it? You think that you've won, don't you? The law can get you yet, and so can I, in a different way.

Maxim Have you anything else to say?

Favell (*smiling*) No. No. I won't keep you.

Favell exits C

Mrs Danvers Shall I be required any more, sir?

Colonel Julyan No, thank you, Mrs Danvers.

Mrs Danvers Then I wish to hand in my notice. I should like to leave Manderley tonight.

Maxim Very well, Mrs Danvers.

Mrs Danvers (*to Colonel Julyan*) You are right about the motive. It is quite clear and plain. Time will never break *that* down. But there are things which may break more easily.

Colonel Julyan I don't understand you, Mrs Danvers.

Mrs Danvers No, sir? I was thinking of Mr de Winter *himself.* Good-night, sir.

Mrs Danvers exits C

Colonel Julyan She can't do anything, nor can Favell. Baker's evidence would squash that. I suppose you never had any idea of this, de Winter?

Maxim No.

Colonel Julyan Well, she was spared the pain at any rate.

Maxim Yes.

Colonel Julyan I don't think it would do any harm if I quietly let it be known in Kerrith what Baker said. Just in case there should be any gossip. People are odd, sometimes. If they knew about Mrs de Winter it might make it a lot easier for you.

Maxim Yes, I understand.

Colonel Julyan (*glancing at his watch*) Crawley. Could you possibly run me home in your car before my daughters send out a search party?

Frank Yes, of course. (*He moves to the double doors*)

Colonel Julyan (*to Maxim*) By the way. (*He looks a little embarrassed*) You didn't have a very long honeymoon, did you? Why not get away for a bit? Take another holiday and go abroad again. No need to hurry back. Crawley will look after things. You could stay away several months. You know the old saying: out of sight, out of mind. Goodbye!

He exits C. *Frank goes with him*

Maxim How much of the truth do you think Julyan guessed? (*He pauses*) He knew. Of course, he knew.

Mrs de Winter If he did, he will never say anything. Never.

Maxim No. (*A pause*) I believe that Rebecca lied to me about the child on purpose. She wanted me to kill her. That's why she was smiling as she died ... She foresaw the whole thing.

Mrs de Winter Maxim, we've got to forget it. We must not think about it any more. It's all over, darling. It's finished.

Maxim You'd better tell them to do your packing tonight. We can drive to London first thing in the morning. If we leave early we shall be able to catch the four o'clock train to Dover. We'll go back to our hotel in Venice. You loved it, didn't you? We'll be happy there. We'll forget everything that's happened.

Mrs de Winter stands very straight and still

What's the matter?

Mrs de Winter Don't you understand? Those words of Mrs Danvers weren't a threat, they were a challenge. Of course, there's going to be malice and gossip, of course there's going to be a scandal. But you can't run away.

Maxim We must go away. Life here will be impossible.

Mrs de Winter But, Maxim ...

Maxim I'm thinking of the people on the estate, who've known me since I was born. They'll have lost all respect, they won't trust me any more.

Mrs de Winter Maxim, you've always taken that for granted. Now you've got to win it back. You can — but not if you run away. They are the real Manderley, aren't they? All the people in the farms and cottages. They mean more to you, don't they, than your own personal pride?

Maxim Are you saying this for your own sake or only for mine?

Mrs de Winter Not for my sake or for yours, but because I believe it to be true.

Maxim We've changed places, haven't we? You, who were so scared and uncertain when you came to Manderley. You're not afraid any more.

Mrs de Winter I'm not afraid because I'm not alone. We're together now. We have no secrets from each other.

Frith enters c

Frith Excuse me, madam, will you be changing, or shall we serve dinner right away?

Mrs de Winter We'll have dinner at once, Frith; we shan't be changing tonight.

Frith Thank you, madam. (*He hesitates, then continues*) Forgive me, madam, but Mr Crawley mentioned something about you and Mr de Winter possibly going abroad.

Mrs de Winter Our plans are uncertain. You must ask Mr de Winter.

There is a pause

Frith I only asked, sir, so as to be able to give the necessary orders in due course.

Maxim does not reply for a moment

Maxim (*slowly and carefully*) As Mrs de Winter said, our plans are uncertain.

A flickering red glow suddenly comes up on the terrace

Good God! (*He pauses momentarily*) There's a fire in the west wing!

Voices (*off, from the garden*) Fire!

Mrs de Winter exits through the french windows, followed by Frith

A firebell sounds. More voices are heard crying across the lawns. Smoke begins to billow up from the terrace and the red light increases

Servants pass on the terrace and in the outer hall

There is the noise of timbers burning

Frith enters through the french windows

Frith (*to Maxim*) Come along, sir, it's spreading!

Frith exits

The tumult outside increases and smoke billows into the hall and on to the upper landing. Maxim turns and begins to move slowly to the staircase. The flickering red light spreads across the hall

Mrs de Winter enters through the french windows

Mrs de Winter Maxim!

Maxim halts, swaying in the smoke. Mrs de Winter crosses quickly to him, puts her arms about him and leads him out through the french windows into the garden

The flickering red light, smoke and the sounds of destructive fire increase within the hall; it will soon be an inferno

Mrs Danvers appears at the top of the staircase and is glimpsed for a moment, her face triumphant, before —

—— *the* CURTAIN *falls*

FURNITURE AND PROPERTY LIST

ACT I

SCENE 1

On stage: OUTER HALL
Table

HALL
On mantelpiece: alabaster vase, ornaments
Couches
Armchairs
Tables. *On one*: various drinks, glasses etc. *On another*: telephone
Grand piano
Newspapers and magazines

Off stage: Luggage (**Servants**)
Decanter of sherry, glasses (**Frith**)
Decanter of whisky, glasses (**Robert**)
Evening paper (**Frith**)

SCENE 2

Set: OUTER HALL
Flower arrangement

Off stage: Roses (**Mrs de Winter**)
Three vases on a tray (**Robert**)
Dress box, tied with string, containing white dress (**Mrs Danvers**)

SCENE 3

Set: Festive decorations

Off stage: Four glasses of champagne on a tray (**Frith**)

Personal: **Frank**: watch, eyepatch
              Beatrice: virginity disc

ACT II
SCENE 1

No additional props

SCENE 2

Strike: All flowers and decorations

SCENE 3

Off stage: Diary (**Mrs Danvers**)

Personal: **Favell**: note
              Colonel Julyan: spectacles

LIGHTING PLOT

Practical fittings required: terrace lights in ACT I SCENE 3

One interior with exterior backing

ACT I, SCENE 1

To open: General interior lighting; evening effect on exterior backing

No cues

ACT I, SCENE 2

To open: General interior lighting with mist effect on exterior backing

No cues

ACT I, SCENE 3

To open: General interior lighting; evening effect on exterior backing.
   Terrace lights on

Cue 1   **Beatrice**: "I believe there's the first car."   (Page 30)
             Car headlights shine through french windows

ACT II, SCENE 1

To open: Interior in semi-darkness; complete darkness outside

Cue 2   **Giles** switches on some lights   (Page 32)
             Bring up some lights

ACT II, SCENE 2

To open: General interior lighting; daytime effect on exterior backing

No cues

ACT II, SCENE 3

To open: General interior lighting; evening effect on exterior backing

Cue 3   **Maxim**: " ... our plans are uncertain."   (Page 60)
             Bring up flickering red glow on terrace

Cue 4	Smoke billows up from the terrace *Increase red light*	(Page 61)
Cue 5	**Maxim** moves towards the staircase *Increase spread of red light across hall*	(Page 61)
Cue 6	**Maxim** and **Mrs de Winter** exit *Increase red light*	(Page 61)

EFFECTS PLOT

ACT I

ACT II